VOICES FROM

Some of the teacher-facilitator comments that inspired this book.

Change will always bring tension, but not as much as a team that lacks agreement on basics or a common vision. A facilitator can move a team to embrace challenges in an environment of understood agreements.

—Timothy Coble, French Teacher, Former Chair of World Languages, American School of Doha, Qatar

A personal challenge I faced was feeling confident enough to lead a group of my peers, especially those colleagues that I have worked with for many years. I also felt the tension of convincing colleagues to buy into new ideas if they are comfortable with their set ways of doing things.

—Shani Smith-Ampley, Middle School Teacher, CM Eppes Middle School, Greenville, NC

Active participation of all staff is very important. With HONEST expression, staff should all have a voice, not simply allowing the veteran teachers to dictate the decisions or sway thinking.

—Jason White, Mathematics Instructor, Ypsilanti Community High School, Ypsilanti, MI

Each meeting should create new information that is applicable and time worthy. The key is to imbed time for implementation. Teachers attend meetings that have critical information but if there isn't follow-up or support for implementation, the meeting was useless.

—Jackie Rangel, Department Chair, La Sema High School, Whittier, CA

IT'S YOUR TURN: TEACHERS AS FACILITATORS

A HANDBOOK

Robert Garmston & Carolyn McKanders

MiraVia® The Road To Learning

MiraVia, LLC, Burlington, VT

Follow us @MiraViaP

Every effort has been made to appropriately cite original sources. We apologize for any oversights in obtaining permission and would be happy to rectify them in future printings.

Microsoft, PowerPoint, and Windows are either registered trademarks or trademarks of Microsoft Corporation in the United States and/or other countries.

10 9 8 7 6 5 4 3 2 1

Printed in the United States of America

ISBN 978-0-9981770-5-2 Softcover

MiraVia, LLC
www.miravia.com

To the loves of our lives, Sue Garmston and Ken McKanders, who with their support and encouragement made this book possible.

Acknowledgments

Writing this book has been a journey of connecting, learning, and love. It has come to fruition through generous contributions and tireless support from numerous people around the world. First, we thank Bruce Wellman and Laura Lipton of MiraVia, our publisher, for guidance, patience, and encouragement in seeing the merit of this work as a needed contribution to facilitation literature and to teacher-leaders. We are forever grateful to the Adaptive School Trainers and Leaders of Thinking Collaborative who've helped refine the original facilitation work of Robert Garmston and Bruce Wellman. Many of their strategies have been adapted for use here. Likewise we thank the hundreds of global teacher-leaders we interviewed who voiced the needs and challenges faced when facilitating colleagues, which is the focus and foundation of this book.

We thank those who we cited for enriching the book with their perspectives, research, and facilitation skills. In particular, we are forever indebted to Kendall Zoller for being an energetic and thoughtful friend, constant source of zeal and encouragement, and professional contributor of innovative nonverbal nuances for virtual facilitation.

While many of our family members graciously engaged us in conversations, we are particularly thankful for our daughters Karla McKanders and Wendy Ferguson. Karla, we are thankful for your gentle and patient responses to the many impromptu calls for help from two techno peasants. Wendy, thank you for walking alongside of us for over a year to support clarity, citations, and editing.

Michael Dolcemascolo is a friend, colleague, and sometimes-partner to us in our work with teachers and those who serve teachers in schools in the

United States and abroad. Without hesitation, he graciously offered to assist us with this project as deadlines grew near and energy waned. This became a better book through his eye for detail and structure, advice when we asked, contribution of specific facilitator tools, and editing for meaning and flow. His infectious laugh made the work a pleasure. Michael's insightful listening tested our premises, challenged our thinking, and brought out the best we had to give. To Michael we offer our utmost thanks.

This book is a response to 400 surveys we received from teachers both nationally and internationally. We wish to thank our friend and advocate Bridgett Doogan for help with connecting us to the voices of teacher-leaders in international schools. Christine Zimmerman is a voracious learner and tireless supporter. We are grateful to Christine for disaggregating and categorizing mounds of data, always with a smile.

It truly has truly taken village of wise, giving people to make this book possible. Jane Ellison has been our long-time close friend and thought partner. Jane, much gratitude for your early support with rescuing us by organizing and meticulously editing our first draft. Frances Gipson, who lives and teaches much of what we write about, contributed examples and ideas; Rebecca Fudge kept us "real" and "practical" in regard to the daily lives of teachers in schools; Jim Roussin always pushed our perspectives to view things from new and deeper angles; Ochan Kusuma-Powell invited thoughtful reflections; and others allowed us to borrow ears in the moment, offered ideas, and showered us with encouraging cheers.

We are forever grateful.

—Bob and Carolyn

Table of Contents

Prologue

> Change the way you look at things, and the things you look at change. —Wayne Dyer

We began to sense the need for this book during conversations with teachers and teacher-facilitators in districts we served and conferences we attended. To broaden the parameters of our inquiries, we talked with principals, assistant principals, and heads of schools. We also talked with curriculum specialists, counselors, instructional-support people, and others who facilitate groups but have more limited decision-making authority.

From these discussions, we came to believe that our greatest contribution would be to write a practical, hands-on handbook for teachers who facilitate meetings and workgroups. The content of this book is in direct response to what we learned from the people who do this work.

Tensions Reported by Teacher-Facilitators

Teachers are overworked and underpaid, wrote George Leonard in *Education and Ecstasy* (1968). This statement is still true today but for different reasons: changing demographics, mountains of state and federal requirements, more committee work, emerging curriculums, mindless reporting of administrivia, and recently, Covid-19 restrictions.

Teachers who facilitate meetings face unique challenges pertaining to full-time classroom duties, being a colleague, and periodically leading colleagues in meetings. Grade level and department teams also encounter special dilemmas when just three or four people are in a meeting. How one stays true to the role of facilitator while remaining an active participant in the group is a central issue this book addresses.

Unique Issues

Some pressures are unique to teacher-facilitators because of their position within school hierarchy. Teachers are accountable to principals, principals to superintendents, and superintendents to school boards. When administrators assign unachievable tasks, a facilitator must become a buffer, protecting the energy and morale of a group.

Demands on facilitators are a problem in any facilitated group but are especially difficult in groups in which the person is also a member. A predictable request is, "Tell us what you think." To give your opinion violates a central premise of facilitation: to facilitate (ease the work of) the group and to not influence its outcome. In order to do this, teacher-facilitators must be impartial and unaligned with any specific position. This is possible if armed with the necessary knowledge.

If you facilitate meetings you may have experienced the five essential mindsets that inform productive facilitation. In the introduction you will learn how to use these perspectives to get results, perceive potential, recognize it's not your group, prepare yet improvise, recruit dissimilarities, and profit from conflict.

These mindsets are often a determining factor in a group's productivity and spirit. Facilitators who use these mindsets cultivate sessions that are productive, efficient, and satisfying. The five mindsets become a resource for addressing the most common complaints: not enough time, no buy-in, limited engagement, conflict, varying degrees of follow-through, and burnout.

Like a SWAT Team

This book does not presume to tell readers how to conduct a meeting. A two-year study of 180 teams at Google found there is no single best way to hold a meeting. Neither is there any best composition of an effective team. Rather, the Google study found that what members do in meetings determines their productivity (Duhigg, 2016). Here is what they found.

Google manager Matt Sakaguchi was previously a member of a SWAT (Special Weapons and Tactics) team. He reported that the following five principles, in order of importance, guide both SWAT teams and the best work teams at Google.

Psychological Safety. This is the idea that you can take a personal risk, and it won't be held against you.

Dependability. Google has a very high standard of work. When you collaborate on a project, it is essential that you can depend on teammates to deliver that high standard.

Structure and Clarity. When you add structure and clarity to ineffective teams—meaning everyone understands their meeting roles and responsibilities—effectiveness increases.

Meaning. The job has to be meaningful to the person or company. You need a personal investment in the work in order to be an effective team member in the long-term.

Impact. You want to be able to see the impact of what you're doing. For example, if you're on a sales team, you can see that you're meeting quota. If you are on a grade-level team you want to see evidence of improved student learning.

Google also found that when norms are present within working groups, it makes the difference between effective and ineffective teams. There are two behaviors that all good teams share.

1. Members speak in roughly the same proportion. "As long as everyone got a chance to talk, the team did well," Anita Woolley, the study's lead author, said. "But if only one person or a small group spoke all the time, the collective intelligence declined" (Woolley et al., 2010, pp. 686–688).
2. Members are skilled at intuiting how others feel based on their tone of voice, their expressions, and other nonverbal cues. People on the more successful teams in Woolley's study scored above average on social sensitivity tests. They seemed to know when someone was feeling upset or left out. People on the ineffective teams, in contrast, scored below average. They seemed, as a group, to have less sensitivity toward their colleagues.

(For more information about effective meeting standards and collaboration norms, see Garmston & Wellman, *The Adaptive School: A Sourcebook for Developing Collaborative Groups*).

Collective Intelligence

Woolley and others found three individual-level features that correlate in a statistically significant way to collective intelligence (2010).

1. The greater the social sensitivity of group members, the smarter the group.
2. The more turn-taking within the group, the better the group performed.
3. The more women in the group, the higher the group IQ.

Collective intelligence is a factor that explains a group's performance on a wide variety of tasks (Woolley et al., 2010).

Who This Book Is For

This book is designed for those who facilitate meetings of any size. Anyone who leads meetings, teaches about meetings, or guides teachers to become better facilitators can benefit. Those who attend meetings as part of their duties can also find value here, as in many cases the knowledge and actions of participants are as important as the facilitation.

We consistently use the term facilitator to refer to anyone leading a group. Many terms exist for this role: chairperson, convener, and manager. We use the term facilitator to mean one who provides facilitation to a group.

Ways to Read This Book

Our goal is that this book will foster increased confidence and competence for anyone who conducts meetings. Readers will find ways to mitigate the major challenges and tensions facilitators and groups experience. Our aim is to support you in achieving effective meetings throughout a school—in department meetings, grade-level groups, PLCs (professional learning communities), school and district committees, and anywhere educators gather to influence student learning.

This handbook offers the what, why, and how of facilitators supporting groups to become more effective, and participants internalizing the commitments, skills, and practices of productive groups. We address the major tensions and questions teacher-leaders shared with us: getting engagement and buy-in, restoring confidence and efficacy, making meetings productive within the limitations of insufficient time, conflicts and "difficult people," and getting teacher/administrative clarity on decision-making processes.

Whatever your reasons for reading this book (as part of a seminar or on your own), we encourage you to select a reading approach that best serves your interests and needs. The book can be read front to back or sampled in chunks. For example, readers may wish to go directly to the mindset of greatest interest to them. Each chapter provides prompts for reflection and ideas to apply what you just read.

Additional Content

In one addendum, Kendall Zoller presents useful ideas that maximize meeting effectiveness when done virtually on Zoom or other platforms. You will find examples of how facilitator tools used in face-to-face meetings can be used effectively in virtual settings.

In the other addendum, we offer an in-depth primer on one of the most fundamental behaviors of facilitating a group: giving directions.

About the Authors

We've chosen to write about meetings for two reasons. First, we've seen many meetings run by teachers and others whose job description does not include leading groups in planning, decision-making, or student assessment. These people face special challenges, and while they can often be effective, other times they need help. Secondly, teachers in many settings shared sources of intense frustration that ultimately deprive them of the influence they should have on shaping student learning. We describe practical responses to these.

Originally, we came to this work as teachers in public schools: Carolyn in Detroit and Bob in California. We had been members of groups both large and small, had seen joyful successes and disappointing failures, and wondered what made the difference. Then, like many others, we began to assume leadership roles fairly early in our careers: Carolyn as a leader in small group settings and Bob as a chairperson on school committees. Curious about the dynamics of groups, we each sought to learn more about what makes them productive.

INTRODUCTION
Mindsets and Meetings: *Navigate with Empowering Mindsets*

> There are things known and there are things unknown, and in between are the doors of perception. —Aldous Huxley

Likov and Harry regarded the opening statements of this afternoon's facilitator differently. Likov appreciated the way the facilitator started, explained the agenda and outcomes for the day, mentioned why the topic was important, and asked if the participants could live with certain ground rules. Harry became bored, thought all this was a waste of time, and wanted to get on with the work.

Likov and Harry were attending a virtual meeting. Each perceived the opening through a different lens. Their reactions would most likely be similar if the meeting had been a face-to-face encounter like traditional meetings. To be attentive and fully present, Likov needed to know the topic's significance, its context, and the ways the group would work. Harry, on the other hand, wanted action, data, and wanted the work to start. It's normal for individuals to experience the same event differently based on perceptions and mindsets. A well-designed opening to the meeting would meet both needs.

Mindsets inform how we see, understand, and behave. They might inform life in general, or as in this case, a specific context: facilitating meetings. This book explores five facilitation mindsets, each with the potential to make facilitators more effective and empower groups.

Mindsets often emerge from prior experiences in which we felt and were successful. Sometimes they persist even when they are no longer effective. You are invited to consider the mindsets described here and ask yourself: If I don't currently use these, what might I need to do to test and acquire them? These five perspectives are at the foundation of effective work with humans.

The Five Mindsets

See groups as they could be. Viewing groups through a lens of continuous improvement is a hallmark of effective leaders. Being seen as having potential stimulates in people a desire to improve and work toward greater effectiveness. This is true for students. This is also true for adults in work groups.

Just as a toddler's first sentence—even though untimely and grammatically flawed—is celebrated, group member conduct can also be appreciated. What facilitators say and how they say it reinforces continuing effort and refinement. In Chapter 2 there are practical skills that can be used to convey perceptions of positive intention to groups as well as language choices that stimulate group learning from their experiences.

Groups grant consent. Humans naturally invest energy in managing the impressions others have of them. For group members to feel safe enough to be themselves and willing to follow the directions of a facilitator, they must perceive that the person facilitating is behaving authentically and is competent, confident, and fair. Chapter 2 covers this facilitator authenticity and explains ways to display certainty, which launches a virtuous cycle of increasing acceptance by the group.

Prepare... don't attach. Spontaneity and improvisation are needed to make a well-planned activity go beyond the ordinary. Brilliant performances require attention to the moment, often responding in ways not anticipated while planning. It is you, your personality, and your uniqueness, which give a performance value. Anyone can execute a plan. Only you can make personal connections in the moment with a group and its responses. Don't get stuck with what you planned. Chapter 3 includes ways to improvise when presented with the unexpected.

Diversity enriches. Inability to hear different voices and perspectives is a death knell for a group's effectiveness. In natural ecosystems, diversity enhances quality. It boosts the availability of oxygen among plants. In aquatic environments it helps purify water. Among humans, it increases the range of perceptions, approaches to problem solving, and viability of ideas. Decisions generated by groups that use contributions from diverse members are more successful and longer lasting than resolutions from groups with greater homogeneity. The most productive teams are those that value diversity, seek others' views, explore options from varied perspectives, seek to understand others, respect minority positions, and honor different ways of thinking. Even groups containing both novices and experts make more effective decisions than groups composed of only experts. Chapter 4 looks at why groups with a mix of perspectives, experiences, cultures, and job descriptions achieve substantially better results than more homogeneous groups.

Never let a conflict go to waste. Former Chicago Mayor Rahm Emanuel put it this way: "Never let a serious crisis go to waste. And what I mean by that is it's an opportunity to do things you think you could not do before." Crises can lead to learning by illuminating a problem and initiating a search for solutions. For example, a broken arm on the playground, parents upset by discrimination, or increasing student truancy all create possibilities for positive change. What can be learned? What resolutions can be tried? What innovative practices might be implemented? Chapter 5 considers how crises can become opportunities.

Readers will find the following structure in each mindset chapter:

- Tensions Teachers Identified
- Guiding Principles for This Mindset
- Relevant Information
- Tools for Facilitators
- Processes for Groups
- Reflecting
- Try This
- Looking Back/Looking Ahead

Of course, mindsets are not the only factors that influence our lives. Each person has many filters that influence how they see and experience things. Professional roles, time in career, country of origin, culture, and personal history are just a handful of these. An interaction a person had at breakfast this morning quite possibly plays a part. We chose to organize around mindsets to provide a conceptual structure for exploring the work of teacher-facilitators.

Each mindset has a cognitive, emotional, and behavioral aspect. Just as Carol Dweck's growth and fixed mindsets give shape to human behavior (2016), the five facilitation mindsets do the same for facilitators, with an important distinction. Growth and fixed mindsets set the direction of human behavior, whereas the five mindsets in this handbook offer facilitators unique choices as they work with groups.

More virtual interactions are occurring than ever before, which requires group members to vary how they interact and to hone their skills for different types of interactions. This is true both professionally and in our personal lives. Each facilitator mindset is a method of defining meaning—a perceptual orientation about a group that is expressed by actions, words, and activities, whether in face-to-face or in virtual meetings.

Two Premises

There are two premises central to successful facilitation. As facilitators incorporate these into their work, situations that previously evoked resistance no longer do. Additionally, facilitators gain understanding of why others react to them the way they do.

The most important premise is that *people have positive intentions.* This premise protects a facilitator from judging, which in turn allows them to be resourceful. At the same time, the other party gains greater access to their own resources

To presume positive intention does not require that you *know* the other person's intentions. Indeed, the other party's motivations may even be unknown or unclear to *them*. But all behaviors are, in some way, attempts to protect oneself. A person who does not reveal information may be protecting their public image. A group that blames others may not feel safe enough to reveal their uncertainties.

Under this premise, we must choose the most generous interpretations. Each person's behaviors are rational, according to their view of reality. To respond with assumptions of positive intention removes resistance, lowers tension, and helps in-the-moment transactions to be productive.

Assuming a person is well-intended evokes a response aligned with that perspective. When we don't understand each other, inquiring about the other's perspective—then listening attentively—brings common understandings from which we can work effectively.

People choose behaviors (even counterproductive, dumb, or hurtful ones) to take care of themselves in the moment. That's because people make the best choices *available to them,* and sound choices are not always perceived. Emotional flooding, for example, can interfere with rational thought. Within that context, yelling is just an attempt to be heard.

A second premise is that the *internal states of people are understood without words.* These psychological states are more influential than the social messages carried by words. Psychological states are communicated somatically – that is, with the body. Internal realities are communicated with facial expressions, tone of voice, gestures, and body language. Often a facilitator may not be aware of these messages. When the psychological message and the social message are incongruent, the "real" message becomes the psychological one. We notice this when a student says she is feeling fine, yet her body is stooped, her face unanimated, and her voice lethargic. You don't need to know the real reason a person is frowning (maybe they are worried about their grandmother). Just presume it is an effort to care for themselves. And be aware of the messages you send. We catch more flies with honey than with vinegar.

Imagine a group unanimously agreeing to an action. Their affirmative vote does not indicate genuine agreement unless their nonverbal signals also say yes. After noticing incongruence, a facilitator may need to gather more information by: 1) informing the group that their faces say one thing and their words another, 2) asking what's going on, 3) suggesting listing some ways this decision could backfire or some possible danger signals as the decision is implemented, or 4) asking "If you were to sabotage this, how would you do it?"

Chapter 1 will illustrate the presumption of positive intent as a foundation for viewing groups at their potential. This in turn creates a Pygmalion effect in which high expectations lead to improved performance. Additionally, readers will find illustrations of ways facilitators use non-verbal language to increase members' comfort.

CHAPTER 1
See A Group As It Could Be: *You Must Perceive It To Achieve It*

Viewing groups through a lens of continuous improvement is a hallmark of effective leaders.

Challenges are when there is an unwillingness to reflect and take ownership of beliefs and actions. Also when there is a lack of skill needed for [accomplishing] the goal of meeting outcomes.

—Instructional Coach, Michigan

One challenge is that there is not an agreed upon set of expectations/ norms. We have a list of norms, but we don't discuss them, and the list is way too long. Also there needs to be self-reflection on the norms at the end of each meeting so that people are aware of how they can improve.

—Teacher-Leader, Near East South Asia Council of Overseas Schools (NESA)

I think it would be useful for teachers to know that there are processes to meetings that can make them highly effective. Taking time to build trust and rapport is also vitally important.

—Teacher, Pitt County Schools Teacher-Leadership Institute, North Carolina

Tensions Teachers Identified

- How should I begin to facilitate a group to get desired outcomes?
- How can I have patience for and a positive attitude toward a developing group?
- What are strategies for growing a group?
- How do I promote productive behaviors in group members?
- How can I trust others to follow through on tasks?
- How do I support groups in setting goals and assessing progress?
- How do I get people to try new things and be open-minded?
- What are strategies for maximizing a group's effectiveness?
- How can I get the group focused on the work versus on me as the facilitator?

See a Group as It Could Be Principles for This Mindset

1. Humans respond in the manner in which they are perceived.
2. Information processed outside a person's awareness is often received and understood more clearly than words.
3. Nonverbal social information is understood with greater accuracy than symbolic messages (including words).
4. Groups seen as becoming more effective experience lower blood pressure, which releases internal resources for growth (Fredrickson, 2009).
5. Seeing oneself as improving is associated with rising performance.
6. The unconscious is always listening (Erickson).

Relevant Information

Viewing groups through a lens of continuous improvement is a hallmark of effective leaders. This growth mindset presumes that individual and group attributes, such as knowledge and skills, can positively change over time.

One cannot pretend to have a growth mindset. A knowledgeable facilitator must adopt certain ways of thinking for success and is aware that neurobiological influences draw all humans toward becoming better and more effective. "Every person's story is about moving towards wholeness. Forward-looking professional development programs know and support this" (Costa & Garmston, 2016, p. 104). The facilitator also accepts that human intentions are positive, even when behaviors may be counterproductive. Beliefs, not behaviors, are the essential element when acting on this mindset, because humans have the capacity to detect incongruence between intention and deed.

When facilitating a meeting, seeing a group as it could be is using a growth—as opposed to a fixed—mindset (Dweck, 2016). This perspective frames events as phases of development akin to a toddler walking. The child wobbles forward, nearly falls, rights themself, and we smile and applaud. We know this is not the end of the toddler's capacity, but simply a current expression of growth initiated in a period of approval and encouragement.

Facilitators support group movement toward potential by introducing mechanisms for self-development. When teams set goals both for themselves and for students and monitor and modify their efforts, they generate a virtuous cycle of continuous growth (Garmston & Wellman, 2016). The team can achieve a collective mindset of growth which further stimulates group efforts at development (Donohoo, 2017; Losada & Heaphy, 2004). It is reasonable to assume that self-directed work improvement increases the rate of collective improvement (Zimmerman et al., 2020). Knowing this, a facilitator allots part of the group's time for development and refinement. Both formal and informal assessment procedures are used.

In addition, Goddard, Hoy, and Woolfolk Hoy (2004) note that in schools where teachers have the opportunity to influence important decisions, they also tend to have stronger belief in their ability to achieve related results. Facilitators can help groups identify where they have decision-making authority and can invite influence or recommendations otherwise.

A second area in which facilitators can enable growth is by being proactive around morale. Facilitators influence morale by what they say and do. Proactive behaviors become essential in periods of crisis or conditions that require adaptivity. It is not unusual for leaders to seek mentoring to help them stay grounded and remain positive in their interactions with others.

Leader influence animates positive member interactions (Finger & Flanagan, 2005), and mindsets influence what leaders say and do. When leaders see groups for their potential, groups perform at higher levels than they otherwise might. A classic Pygmalion experiment proved this to be true. In the experiment, elementary teachers were told that certain students would be "intellectual bloomers" and outperform classmates. And then they did. In pre- and post-testing the experimental group showed a mean gain in IQ (Rosenthal & Jacobson, 1968). The essence of the study is that high expectations lead to improved performance. Expect more, get more. The converse—expect less and get less—is also true (Eden, 2018).

Barbara Frederickson (2001) attributes results like these to her "broaden and build" theory. First, positive emotions challenge and set aside negative explanations we might have for the behavior of others. Next, we become aware of a range of positive ways to respond beyond what might have otherwise occurred to us. We become primed to look for creative, flexible ways of thinking and acting. Generously interpreting the behavior of others supports growth.

For some time, researchers including Losada & Heaphy (2004), Fredrickson (2001, 2009, 2013), and Gottman (2005) have found positivity related to higher performance. Gottman's studies of couples, Losada's research with business teams, and Fredrickson's examinations of ways the body reacts to positivity or negativity have confirmed the values of positivity. Fredrickson observed that negativity could spike blood pressure whereas positivity can calm it, working like a thermometer for the body and brain. The effects of positivity geometrically multiply.

A third dimension supporting growth is recognizing that social interactions activate the same threat and reward responses in our brain that we rely on for physical survival (Rock, 2020). Rock's work identifies five areas of human need: 1) feeling comfortable with our relative importance to others (status), 2) a sense of certainty about predicting the future (certainty), 3) a sense of control over events (autonomy), 4) feeling connected to other people (relatedness), and 5) feeling we are being treated fairly (fairness). Pinker (2008) observes that language conveys messages to other people, and at the same time it negotiates the social relationship between the speaker and receiver. For example, a facilitator might point to a chart and say, "Look this way," or "Please look this way." The instruction is the same but the second is more polite, conveying a more equitable relationship between facilitator and group.

Status, certainty, autonomy, relatedness, and fairness are trigger points for humans. When we feel threatened by a topic, conversation, or what is said, the hormone cortisol is released, which diminishes creativity and productivity. In contrast, the brain releases oxytocin, the "happy hormone," when we relate with others in positive ways. This promotes a feeling of well-being.

This might explain why an unexpected emotional response could result from an interaction with a group member or facilitator. In groundbreaking research about teams at Google, psychological safety was found to be the first, and most essential, ingredient for team effectiveness (Duhigg, 2016). Other studies have borne this out (Edmundson, 2019).

Social messages are received both consciously and beyond our awareness. Messages of regard received outside of our awareness are recognized as much or more than messages received consciously. Since we cannot evaluate what we are not conscious of, messages received subconsciously are accepted as true. Presuppositions in language influence perception. We know from legendary therapist Milton Erickson that the unconscious is always listening. Unlike the conscious mind, however, the unconscious has no filters to interpret, generalize, or distort information. The brain is bombarded with eleven million bits of information per second (DiSalvo, 2013; Kwong, 2020). But the brain can only process forty to sixty bits per second, so we have an unimaginable amount of data bombarding us that we cannot consciously process.

Consciously, we detect insincerity, prevarication, and prejudices, and we are able to detect these not only from language but also from non-verbal signals we receive. We can do this because we focus on what seems most important at a specific moment. The rest is deleted from our conscious awareness.

Social messages that can either wound or celebrate us are often conveyed by what the speaker supposes but does not directly say. Such presuppositions are received subconsciously and slip undetected through the brain's filtering systems (Costa & Garmston, 2016). Someone posing the question "Given your commitment to fair treatment, what ideas might be considered for this situation?" makes several assumptions. First, fair treatment is valued; second, you consider using fairness as a criterion; and third, you are a fair-minded group and thus are honorable. Since these messages are received out of consciousness, and therefore not scrutinized, they are taken for granted.

Facilitators, seeing a group as it could be, convey this positive orientation through attentiveness to morale, initiating self-directed improvement activities, being sensitive to social messages, and using presuppositions.

Human behavior is driven by a need to take care of ourselves. Behaviors we choose, consciously or instinctively, are motivated by self-preservation. They are positively intended, even if at times counterproductive, and are informed by filters derived from experiences, emotions, inner conflicts, and beliefs. The brain deletes, distorts, and generalizes information and leaves us with a condensed and altered version of all that surrounds us—an internal interpretation of reality. Since most people are not consciously aware of their subconscious filters, they're also unaware that their view of the world is basically "made up." This also means that whatever you think you are is only a fraction of the truth.

TOOLS FOR FACILITATORS

To see a group as it could be, facilitators choose tools that help the group see themselves in a positive light by being self-directed and successful.

WHAT: **Positive Presuppositions**

WHY: Convey the facilitator's mindset with indirect messages of capability, positive intentions, and/or self-empowerment.

HOW: Ask: "Given your wish for greater efficiency, how open might you be to experiment with this?"

In this example, presuppositions include that:

1. the group desires efficient use of time,
2. some openness exists,
3. this is just a test—you are not committed to continued use.

TIME:	GROUP SIZE:	MATERIALS:
Less than a minute	Any	None

WHAT: **Third Point**

WHY: Focus on the work instead of on the facilitator or one another.

HOW: Get the group to look at a visual (on a screen or flip chart) by using a frozen hand gesture pointed toward the visual and directing your own eyes at it. The group's eyes go where the facilitator's eyes go.

TIME:	GROUP SIZE:	MATERIALS:
Less than a minute	Any size	Flip chart or screen with a visual on it

WHAT: **Closing the Window**

WHY: Alert that the time for a conversation on a given topic is ending.

HOW: The facilitator says, "You have this much time left on this topic," while holding hands a shoulder width apart and slowly moving them closer together.

Tips:

- Move hands slowly together while scanning the group for any signals that someone wants to speak.
- This strategy may stimulate contributions from people who have been sitting on an idea but have not yet said it.

TIME:	GROUP SIZE:	MATERIALS:
Less than a minute	Any	None

WHAT: **Pluses and Wishes**

WHY: Assess ways the group is working, and provide data for future improvement.

HOW: Record responses to "What's a plus for today?" in the left column on a flip chart. Asking "What else?" carries a presupposition that more is to come. Avoid asking "Anything else?" which can be answered yes or no and will often end the data collection. Then ask, "What's a wish for today or the next time we meet? What might we have done more of, less of, or differently?" Record wishes in right hand column.

TIME:	GROUP SIZE:	MATERIALS:
About 8 minutes	3+	Markers and flip chart or whiteboard

WHAT: **What-Why-How Pattern**

WHY: Whenever presenting a group with a process, offering clarity about "what" they will be doing—naming it—is both respectful and facilitates clear communication. Follow with a "why"—the purpose, rationale, even research, if appropriate—which treats the group as thoughtful participants and partners. Finally, offer the "how"—the directions or steps for the task—in a visual way whenever possible so adults feel competent and resourceful as the process proceeds (Lipton & Wellman, 2011).

HOW: Here's an example of a facilitator using the What-Why-How pattern for a brainstorming session.

- **What:** "The next step is to brainstorm."
- **Why:** "As you know, the purpose of brainstorming is to get as many ideas on the table as possible. Questions or comments derail the process, leading to a more limited and less useful list."
- **How:** "I'll record the ideas on this chart paper. When you raise your hand, I will give you a number to place you in a queue, so you know you'll have a turn and not worry about being able to add your idea. If you have a question or comment, hang on to it. We will come back to it in the next step."

TIME:	GROUP SIZE:	MATERIALS:
1–2 minutes	Any	None

PROCESSES FOR GROUPS

To see a group as it could be, facilitators choose processes that help the group see themselves in a positive light by being self-directed and successful.

WHAT: **Group Visioning**

WHY: Begin with the end in mind and set goals for maximum effectiveness.

HOW: Begin a meeting by offering a conversation prompt such as: "How might we know that we (you)* are operating well?" or "What might we (you)* look like and sound like when we (you)* are performing at our best?" Chart responses.

*Use "we" if you are part of the group, and "you" if you are an external facilitator.

TIME:	GROUP SIZE:	MATERIALS:
5–10 minutes	3+	Markers and flip chart or whiteboard

WHAT: **I'm In**

WHY: Maximize effectiveness by confirming each member's readiness to participate.

HOW: Round-Robin. Each person says something on their mind about a topic of their choice: their classroom, this group, expectations for today, an event like a field trip, etc., or simply, "I'm in."

TIME:	GROUP SIZE:	MATERIALS:
4–6 minutes	3+	Markers and flip chart or whiteboard

WHAT: **Two Sides of a Coin**

WHY: Promote productive behaviors.

HOW: Work with a partner or assign small groups. Hand out index cards. On one side, each person writes a word that expresses how they want to feel at the end of the seminar/session/meeting. Round-Robin share that side of the card. Next, on the other side, each person writes a short phrase for "self-talk" that they will use to guide their choices today and support them in achieving outcomes. Round-Robin share side two. (Developed by Bruce Wellman).

TIME:	GROUP SIZE:	MATERIALS:
10 minutes	Rearrange into groups of 4–6	Index cards, pens

WHAT: **Group Reflections**

WHY: Supports groups in setting goals and assessing progress.

HOW: Ask "How did we do with our working agreements?" or "How did we do with managing time?" or "How did we do with staying on the agenda?" etc.

TIME:	GROUP SIZE:	MATERIALS:
5–7 minutes	Rearrange into groups of 4–6	None

WHAT: **Group Inventory**

WHY: Promote productive behaviors with self-directed reflection.

HOW: Members respond to an inventory similar to the example below. Data is collated and presented. Dialogue culminates in identifying selected areas to improve. Tip: Schedule the dialogue for the next meeting.

Group Inventory worksheet available for download at: https://bit.ly/2VFNhZZ

TIME:	GROUP SIZE:	MATERIALS:
5–7 minutes	Rearrange into groups of 4–6	Group Inventory worksheet

Decide On Decision-Making

We were clear about who we are in the decision making process.

LOW —1—— 2—— 3—— 4—— 5— HIGH

We were clear about what decision making processes are being used.

LOW —1—— 2—— 3—— 4—— 5— HIGH

Develop Standards

We adhered to one process at a time.

LOW —1—— 2—— 3—— 4—— 5— HIGH

We adhered to one topic at a time.

LOW —1—— 2—— 3—— 4—— 5— HIGH

We balanced participation.

LOW —1—— 2—— 3—— 4—— 5— HIGH

The degree to which I felt listened to.

LOW —1—— 2—— 3—— 4—— 5— HIGH

The degree to which I listened to others.

LOW —1—— 2—— 3—— 4—— 5— HIGH

We engaged in productive cognitive conflict.

LOW —1—— 2—— 3—— 4—— 5— HIGH

We were clear about meeting roles today.

LOW —1—— 2—— 3—— 4—— 5— HIGH

Reflecting

Take a moment by yourself or with a colleague to consider these questions.

1. As you reflect upon your own continuous improvement as a facilitator, who might be a resource you could rely upon for coaching, goal setting, and planning meetings?
2. How might you use, for example, the maps of Cognitive Coaching^{SM} (Costa & Garmston, 2016) as scaffolds for those conversations?
3. As you listen to others speak, what do you notice about the positive presuppositions embedded in their language? Given your own language patterns, what might be a possible next step for you?

Try This

1. Over time, administer the Meeting Inventory offered in this chapter several times. Share the data with the group and analyze patterns. Conclude with group goal-setting based on the data.
2. After completing the Pluses & Wishes charting at the conclusion of a meeting, organize the feedback into categories. Present the information to the group at the beginning of the next meeting and have them construct meaning from the data.
3. In your next meeting, practice using Third Point, perhaps to explain the posted agenda.

Looking Back/Looking Ahead

Data show that growth-focused groups have higher satisfaction and are more productive than groups without this orientation. Growth-focused facilitation supports the group's resourcefulness and frames present-moment observations within a larger context as steps towards the group's goal. A leader facilitating from this perspective frames the group's growth as unfolding over time, accepts and supports the group's learning from reflection and practicing better ways of working, assumes positive intentions of the members, and monitors and processes the group's goals. Envisioning a group as it could be sets the stage, granting the facilitator consent to authentically lead meetings. This is the foundation for building trust and safety within the group and moving towards the second mindset—groups grant consent.

Chapter 2 will explore the importance of perception, but this time from the vantage point of group members. What the group believes to be true about the facilitator will influence the facilitator's effectiveness and the group's success.

CHAPTER 2
Groups Grant Consent: *Get Permission to Lead*

Groups must perceive the facilitator as behaving authentically, and as competent, confident, and fair.

Major tensions are egos and my feeling self-conscious about my ability to be respected. Teachers sometimes don't take what I say seriously because I'm not their administrator.

—Grade 4 Teacher and Literacy Coach, Michigan

Trying to make meetings meaningful and useful to the teachers in my department. I want them to feel that it is a good use of their time and that they are getting something out of it, but most of the time, the agenda is set for me by the principal so I mostly cover "nuts and bolts" instead of getting into the teaching and learning.

—Department Chair, Near East South Asia Council of Overseas Schools

When you do not have the "role authority" in facilitating meetings, it can be a challenge to move forward on changes in district programs. You need administrative authority which can be difficult to coordinate.

—Department Chair, Midwestern United States

Tensions Teachers Identified

- How can we be seen as authentic when facilitating?
- How do we communicate confidence and competence?
- How do we overcome personal butterflies?
- How can we avoid being perceived as messengers of the administration?
- How do we help group members feel that a meeting is useful?
- How do we acquire a greater range of facilitation skills?
- How do we communicate prompt and clear purposes during end-of-day meetings?
- How do we generate trust in meeting processes?
- How can we be clear who is facilitating meetings during which everyone is seated?

Groups Grant Consent
Principles for This Mindset

1. Group members need confidence in a facilitator in order to be fully engaged in a meeting.
2. First impressions set the direction for a meeting.
3. Groups respond to what they perceive, rather than to what is.
4. Behaviors that convey confidence can be learned.
5. What leaders do and how they speak communicates more confidence than what they say.
6. Facilitators can establish and maintain a safe environment.
7. Psychological safety is essential for effective group work.

Relevant Information

When a facilitator appears confident and competent, the psychological safety of the group is enhanced. Teams will experiment with ideas, regard collective learning as normal, value diversity, and recognize the contributions of others when they feel safe. In these settings periods of reflection may be structured around these questions: What are we learning? What can we do better? What should we change? (Zimmerman, et al., 2020).

Teams in which teachers feel safe tend to trust leadership and accept direction without feeling manipulated or controlled. A group's consent to be facilitated is essential for facilitation to occur. Groups grant this permission when they sense the facilitator is behaving authentically, is in charge, and when they feel the setting is safe. Crafting a safe meeting involves clarity about roles and using familiar structures such as opening routines, agenda formats, and progress assessments. Certain facilitator behaviors are important to a safe environment. Among these are attentive listening, impartiality and patience, sensitivity to group energy, and keeping the goal in sight (Hanifan, 2020). Brene Brown, a University of Houston professor, author, and vulnerability and courage guru, suggests that facilitator-leader vulnerability also contributes to a group feeling secure (2018).

At the beginning of a teaching career, feeling unnatural is natural. "Do I look like a teacher?" Many teachers confess to this initial feeling. We too experienced this during our first days as teachers. Teacher-leaders may feel similar apprehensions or awkwardness when they first facilitate groups of colleagues, since relationships may shift. In these situations, teacher facilitators may invest energy presenting a complimentary image of themselves, and attention is directed inward instead of out to the group. Being oneself in new situations enlists confidence in what you do. If you trade your authenticity for safety, you may experience anxiety and limits on your effectiveness (Brown, 2018). When this occurs, artificial behaviors emerge and are transparently obvious to others.

Humans naturally invest energy in managing the impressions others have of them. In doing so, we appear as less than we are, and this lack of authenticity is both noticed and withdraws a portion of trust. To be vulnerable is to be who we are, warts and all. "Our ability to be daring leaders will never be greater than our capacity for vulnerability" (Brown,

2018, p. 11). Brown advocates that people develop vulnerability skill sets to help overcome uncertainties natural to taking on a new role. Saying things such as, "I hope you can bear with me on this. I've not done this before and I'm working my way through it," or "I intend to listen to each person. If you think I am not understanding someone, please let me know."

Even if one is skillful, if the group does not see it that way they will resist efforts to be facilitated. While a facilitator's confidence and competence are essential to leadership, these qualities do not matter if not perceived by the group. It is for this reason that using rehearsed patterns during an initial introduction to a group or the first session of a meeting is useful. When performing a rehearsed opening, confidence and comfort grow. Competence will develop with continuous learning, experience, and reflection on experience (Garmston & Wellman, 2016). Consistent personal assessment, goal setting, and patience with oneself are hallmarks of a healthy personal growth mindset in any role.

Facilitators need general communication skills, but these are not enough. Facilitation requires the special skill sets of a coach, a counselor, or a Socratic teacher. A strong facilitator's questions are open-ended, they listen reflectively, their messages convey positive presuppositions, and their voice patterns are congruent with the intention of their message. Grinder (1993) found that in classrooms, vocal variety—variation in pitch, tempo, intensity, and tonal quality—results in increased comprehension. This is also true in adult meetings (Zimmerman, et. al., 2020). Facilitators, teachers, and administrators change the meaning of messages by altering tone or gestures. Different messages are conveyed by different ways of using voice. This appears to be universal.

Zoller (2007) conducted a video study of teachers in five languages. In every classroom, the teacher demonstrated two voice patterns, with students responding in kind. One was represented by a flat, decreasing rhythm (a credible voice), and another by a different, more rhythmic voice pattern (approachable voice). These nonverbal patterns persisted in all five languages with minor differences in frequency and range.

One voice tone invites comment and another gives information. A voice tone that is rhythmic and ranges up and down in pitch is considered approachable, as it invites the listener to respond. This *approachable voice* encourages participation. When the speaker uses a narrower, flatter pitch range, however, and drops the voice at the end, the listeners ready themselves to receive information or direction. This *credible voice* pattern is a voice of command or direction, and listeners know they are expected to agree. We advocate the practice of this use of voice so that comfort and confidence are achieved.

Facilitators use the credible voice when wanting to be definitive, when giving directions, and to establish credibility (Garmston & Zimmerman, 2013). The alternate approachable voice, with greater range and rhythm, signals the speaker is seeking a response.

Universally, humans want to know they have been heard and that the listener is attempting to understand. Paraphrasing is reported to be the most influential verbal tool used by effective facilitators, teachers, administrators, and parents. Paraphrasing builds trust.

> Paraphrasing honors another person's communication. Just as when people feel they are being understood, they breathe more deeply, which provides more oxygen to the brain, which is essential for thinking. At another level, a series of empathic paraphrasing changes blood chemistry and helps to keep the person being coached in a resourceful state (Zimmerman, et al., 2020, p. 96).

Acknowledging also lets people know they are heard. "Thank you" is enough, and carries an aura of respect for the speaker and the group.

Facilitator confidence increases along with credibility when meetings are perceived as meaningful. Displaying and stating a clear meeting purpose is a foundation of a productive meeting. Inviting members to articulate how they understand the goals and to comment on how to make the purpose more relevant supports trust, buy-in, and safety.

Effective facilitators are clear about their role, its boundaries, and its responsibilities, and they distinctly communicate this to groups. This includes clarity regarding confidentiality, information reporting and sharing, and decision-making authority and protocols. Often decision-making authority must be clarified with those who have role authority, such as a principal.

TOOLS FOR FACILITATORS

Because *groups grant consent* to be facilitated, facilitators choose tools that convey confidence and craft a safe environment.

WHAT: **Attention First**

WHY: Both Grinder (1993) and Zoller (2010) strongly advocate that attention should always be the first order of business. This uses time efficiently and decreases frustration for both speaker and listeners.

HOW: To gain the group's attention, the facilitator will do the following:

- Assume a credible stance: feet parallel, hip distance apart, stand still.
- Be still—freeze the posture.
- Announce in a credible voice, "Look this way please."
- Hold the posture until almost all members are silent and focused.
- Conclude with "Thank you," stated in a credible voice.
- When the group is attentive and still, break eye contact, breathe, and step into a new stance. Again, with a credible voice, give the next direction.

TIME:	GROUP SIZE:	MATERIALS:
1 minute	Any	None

WHAT: **Hand Signal**

WHY: As groups tire, group members often respond less to verbal directions. During a working session we often use a hand signal to redirect attention from small group conversation to full group work. The visual nature of this strategy gets attention from those who process visually, and their silence alerts auditory processors to pay attention (Garmston & Wellman, 2002).

HOW: Assume a credible stance, stand still, and hold one hand in the air as a prearranged signal for silence. As group members notice the gesture they copy it, signaling to those who may not have noticed that you need their attention.

TIME:	GROUP SIZE:	MATERIALS:
1–2 minutes	Any	None

WHAT: **Facilitator Rituals**

WHY: To boost confidence and aid presence.

HOW: Facilitator rituals might include arriving at a consistent time before the group, arranging chairs for sight lines, distributing sticky notes and other working materials, or charting a public agenda before the meeting. Facilitators may send an agenda, working agreements, and any necessary meeting materials ahead of time. If working virtually, they might check lighting, camera, and arrange notes for easy access.

TIME:	GROUP SIZE:	MATERIALS:
Depends on chosen rituals	Any	Might include furniture, tech, charts, handouts, notes, and supplies.

WHAT: **Role Clarification**

WHY: Being explicit about the facilitator's role in a meeting/session.

HOW: Facilitators introduce themselves to the group and indicate that their job is to support the group in getting its work done. Facilitators providing basic facilitation will specify that their services are to do the following:

- Monitor time and guide processes.
- Be impartial to content.
- Intervene when processes interfere with the group achieving its goals.

A facilitator providing developmental facilitation, in which the group will accomplish a task while improving its effectiveness, will specify that their services are to do the following:

- Monitor time and guide processes.
- Be impartial to content.
- Intervene when processes are interfering with the group achieving its goals, when processes or factors hinder the long-term effectiveness of the group, or when reflecting on process will help group resilience and skills.
- A facilitator interacting as a team member and providing facilitation within small groups-perhaps 3 people-will sit, and then stand up to perform leadership functions.

TIME:	GROUP SIZE:	MATERIALS:
2–3 minutes	Any	None

WHAT: **Decision-Making Guiding Questions**

WHY: Clarity about decision-making is one of the most critical functions influencing meeting success. Often group members are not clear about who is making final decisions and what decision-making process will be used. It is important that people trust the process.

HOW: Facilitator and group members have clarity on the answers to these five guiding questions:

- What topics are ours?
- Who decides?
- Who are we in the decision-making process?
- What decision-making process will be used?
- When and how will the decision be communicated?

TIME:	GROUP SIZE:	MATERIALS:
1–2 minutes	Any	None

WHAT: **Public Agenda**

WHY: Shared ownership and understanding of the meeting topics.

HOW: Create charted agenda, using alternating colors and possibly incorporating "ChartArt."* Present at beginning of meeting, and reference periodically throughout the meeting to indicate what's been covered and what's coming up ("Station Naming"). Ask, "What items might we need to add to the agenda?" at the beginning of the meeting and "What items might we consider for our next meeting?" at the conclusion. (*Reproducible designs for charting available from www.miravia.com).

TIME:	GROUP SIZE:	MATERIALS:
10 minutes to create, 5 minutes to share	Any	Chart paper, markers, ChartArt (optional)

PROCESSES FOR GROUPS

Because *groups grant consent*, facilitators choose processes that convey confidence and craft a safe environment.

WHAT: **Prioritizing Outcomes**

WHY: Personal and group ownership, as well as seeing relevance of meeting outcomes.

HOW: Facilitator presents outcomes using a visual as a Third Point (see Facilitator's Tools, Chapter 1). Then ask group members to turn to a partner and share which outcome seems most relevant to them and why. Switch, paraphrase the first partner and add. Conclude with first partner paraphrasing the second.

TIME:	GROUP SIZE:	MATERIALS:
2–3 minutes	Any	Visual of outcomes

WHAT: **Stand-Up Meeting**

WHY: Time is precious, and an item is "hot."

HOW: Convene meeting in a space with no chairs. Stand, circling a chart stand with one-item agenda visible to all. Indicate clear purpose: decision, action, next direction, etc. At conclusion, pairs summarize meeting outcome to check for understanding.

TIME:	GROUP SIZE:	MATERIALS:
10–15 minutes	4–12	Chart stand with chart paper or whiteboard

WHAT: **Group Choice**

WHY: Maintaining group efficacy and autonomy.

HOW: Show an agenda and invite group to add items and to number the order in which items will be addressed. In terms of decisions, have clarity on group's role: to inform, recommend, or decide. (See Decision-Making Guiding Questions on p. 29) For timing, get group's input on when to break, meeting dates, etc. Seek to have three or more alternatives for choice-making, and consistently look for opportunities to give the group options/choice.

TIME:	GROUP SIZE:	MATERIALS:
10–15 minutes	Any	Agenda, markers

WHAT: **One-2-Six**

WHY: Quickly develop a common group focus.

HOW: Follow these steps.

1. Explain the purpose: "Next we need to be clear about this group's purpose. One way to do this is by generating a short statement that summarizes the central focus of our group."
2. Each person writes one or more drafts in response to a prompt written on a chart. Possible prompts include: "What seems the logical next step in the project?" or "What might we do to resolve [group problem]?" or "What's the best use of our time today?"
3. Pair up participants. They share their drafts and agree on one.
4. Pairs share with two other pairs and agree on one response.
5. Post and organize the final responses.
6. Facilitator guides process for final consensus.

TIME:	GROUP SIZE:	MATERIALS:
15–20 minutes	Any	Flip chart, markers

Reflecting

Take a moment by yourself or with a colleague to consider these questions.

1. What are some things you might do now for personal confidence when preparing to facilitate a meeting (see Facilitator Rituals on p. 27)? What might be useful to add to your repertoire? Who would be a good person to talk with about your interest in this topic?
2. What are you learning about your vocal patterns in terms of credibility and approachability? Which might be your natural default, and what is the stretch for you to expand your skills? Experiment with number 3 below.

Try This

1. Explore ChartArt on the MiraVia website (www.miravia.com), and practice adding color and images to your charts for your next meeting.
2. Using the Decision-Making Guiding Questions tool above, draft an opening speech for your next meeting. Consider recording audio or video of yourself for self-assessment.
3. Extend your range of voice tone and practice your credible and approachable voice. Test it with students.

Looking Back/Looking Ahead

Groups implicitly grant consent to be facilitated when they perceive a leader to be confident, competent, and truthful (Keltner, 2016). Groups quickly make initial impressions of leaders. These impressions, it's been found, continue throughout an engagement. University students, for example, report this experience with professors. Teacher-facilitators must be intentional in their initial actions in order to obtain a group's consent. In this context, the group's perceptions determine the level of facilitator trust and credibility. When facilitators are intentional about setting the group's goals, creating meeting agendas, and fluently opening the meeting, members experience relaxed-alertness as opposed to anxiety.

Facilitators prepare by planning well and remaining flexible while conducting the meeting. Chapter 3 will identify some problems when rigidly sticking to your plan.

Reflecting

CHAPTER 3
Prepare... Don't Attach:
Your Responses Are More Important

Spontaneity and improvisation are needed to make a well-planned meeting go beyond the ordinary.

Challenges are getting off topic and staying focused on the agenda items and making sure that every voice is heard when having a big number of participants.

—Arabic Coordinator and World Language Leader, Amman, Jordan

People want to have an opportunity to share out with the entire group. It is sometimes difficult to say we will share feedback at a later time. How do you stay on track and honor these voices?

—Teacher-Leader/Data Coach, Los Angeles, CA

How long to let stories go on before tying back to the agenda? Sometimes there seems to be a need to allow these personal connections because we don't see each other often.

—Instructional Coach, Midwestern United States

Tensions Teachers Identified

- What should I do when a few members are adamant about wanting to add a new topic to an already crowded agenda?
- What strategies can I use when the direction of the group is different from my own?
- How do I manage when I'm named as the facilitator and arrive to learn there are no goals for the meeting?
- What should I do if midway through a virtual meeting a member loudly proclaims the meeting is BS and refuses to participate?
- How do I manage when the slide deck or videos/visuals for a meeting are corrupted and won't play?
- How do I get buy-in on a topic when teachers are uninformed and confused about why we're discussing it?

Prepare... Don't Attach
Principles for This Mindset

1. Facilitation often requires flexibility in the moment.
2. One important aspect of facilitation is anticipating the need for improvising.
3. The person with the greatest flexibility has the most influence.
4. A group appreciates you more than your plans.
5. We are most fully alive and appreciated when we respond intuitively with ideas, behaviors, and information.
6. Unrehearsed decisions are more likely to be effective when the final goal is in mind.
7. Work consistently toward relationships and outcomes.

Relevant Information

As long as a facilitator has planned well and considered the agenda from the group's perspective, they are unlikely to feel put-upon by unexpected events. However, we've found that the planned agenda is not always the agenda from which to work. Sometimes a disruption occurs that must be addressed. Occasionally we find that moving outside the agenda better suits a group's needs or meeting outcomes. Keeping the original overall outcome in mind allows deviation to occur while still achieving goals.

Like a slender tree bending in a forceful wind, a confident facilitator adjusts to new information or situational changes. A new topic is requested, another topic demands more time than anticipated, a dispute emerges that must be settled in order to address others, an unexpected emergency occurs, a last-minute request is made from administration or an unhappy contingent of parents or teachers, or the darn agenda is just wrong. Under these conditions, a facilitator either bends or breaks. Open-mindedness and flexibility are required to prepare... but not attach to that preparation. It is with these attributes that a facilitator can breathe life into a meeting, be empathic and flexible, and respond in ways that are safe for the group. At these times especially, you are more important than your plan.

Unexpected events are not the only time that going off script is necessary. Our friend Shondra had half a group leave a meeting in the middle of the morning. Fortunately, she was advised ahead of time that a strike action was likely to occur, and she had planned strategies ahead of time to successfully manage the shift.

Basic tools are required to manage disruption. First, pay attention to energy. When one plans well, mental space is available to attend to energy cues such as body positions, voice tones, and breathing.
A second resource is managing one's emotions. Breathing and moving help accomplish this. A couple of deep breaths allow the oxygen required for thinking to enter the brain. It also slows the heart. Third, assign a generous interpretation of what occurred, remembering that people sometimes do unwise things in efforts to take care of themselves.
Fourth, create think time. A number of strategies can accomplish this. Say something like, "Turn to your neighbor and talk about what just happened."

A fifth option is to create movement. Movement changes the mental states of participants and infuses energy into the room. Say something like, "Okay, let's pause. Everyone stand and stretch" or "For some fresh perspectives on this, sit next to someone you haven't talked with today" or "Please form a trio and construct a suggestion to present to the group" or "Let's do a line-up. Those who agree stand on this end; if uncertain stand in the middle, and those who disagree stand on the other end" or "Okay, let's get some energy in the room. Without talking, line up according to the day and month of your birthday." Once people move around, there are many varieties of topics or choices for who to speak with. Finally—and we've done this a number of times—call a break.

Innovation serves the group and can enliven the facilitator. When Martin Luther King Jr. spoke at the March on Washington for Jobs and Freedom in 1963, his friend, singer Mahalia Jackson, was sitting on the platform since she'd just finished her performance. Seven paragraphs into King's speech, Jackson yelled to him, "Tell them about the dream, Martin! Tell them about the dream!" The word "dream" was nowhere in his written remarks because he had used it earlier, unsuccessfully he felt, in Detroit. At Jackson's prompting, King set aside his speech and began improvising.

As one observer described it, King riffed on parts from his earlier speech, on bits from the Bible, Shakespeare, Lincoln, the Constitution, and the Declaration of Independence. What we recall today is the power of his message and the majesty of his voice as he delivered the moving speech we now call "I Have a Dream" on that August day. King improvised, drawing on information he had not prepared to deliver. No longer speaking from notes, he left his agenda and spoke from his heart. We would say he brought himself into the situation.

Participants value you more than the topic or agenda. An agenda is largely passive, whereas your presence is interactive. You can respond, while an agenda cannot. Your open-mindedness contributes to members feeling safe. And you are valued because members have a relationship with you. Whether it is warm, medium, or cool, they have a sense of who you are. A middle-school teacher-facilitator told us that during a recent in-service day, the group went weird. Energy was uncharacteristically low, several people were on their laptops, and attention was mostly absent. Finally he asked, "What's going on here?" They told him today's topic had been covered at the beginning of the year, and while they recognized its value, more urgent things were on their minds. "Okay," the teacher-facilitator said, "what should we be talking about?" They made a necessary change.

You are always more important than your agenda because you have the ability to respond to changing situations, while an agenda cannot. The plans developed by a facilitator, a teacher, a sports team, or any interactive endeavor are just abstractions until you step into the presence of others, able to sense a group's fatigue, excitement, or disappointment. You've entered a responsive world, and you bring three assets: your plan, your contingency ideas, and yourself. Each of us is greater than our plan.

As mentioned before, another indispensable tool is the paraphrase. We once watched a presenter respond to an angry outburst from a teacher. Calmly, she asked his name, moved toward him, paraphrased his complaint, and as if in a dance together, inquired about what she might do to help, offering to talk with him at break. She said, "You're angry because you have to be here and aren't seeing any value for yourself or students. It's a waste of time." He became slightly less rigid. She paraphrased again. You could hear a pin drop in the room.

Paraphrasing disarms, creates clarity for both listener and speaker, deepens understanding, and reveals opportunities for what to do. Indeed, paraphrasing slows the pulse rate of every member during an interchange. Demonstrating cognitive empathy through paraphrasing can extrinsically regulate negative emotions on a short-term basis. Paraphrasing affects emotional states in the direction of feeling better (Seehausen, et al., 2012).

The person with the greatest flexibility has the greatest influence, according to Gregory Bateson (2000). His work cuts across many fields, and he's cited in biodiversity, systems theory, cybernetics, philosophy, anthropology, semantics, and psychology. He relates human flexibility to the law of requisite variety. Requisite—as required—varieties have the capacity to change form while maintaining identity. The most flexible organisms have the most control in their environments.

Flexibility is not a synonym for facilitate, but comes close. A paraphrase is like an aikido move, flexible and resilient. Both emphasize achieving complete mental calm and control of one's responses. Aikido is said to be a way of harmonizing energy. Courtesy and respect are essential aspects. Aikido flows with the energy rushing toward it, just as saying in your own words what you understand another to feel. Paraphrasing is a facilitator's aikido.

What is often needed to address surprises is time. Develop a personal tool set. The first tool is breathing. Take a deep breath, take a few steps in contemplation, inhale, and hold it for a bit at the top of the inhale. Repeat. Oxygen floods your brain, necessary for thinking. Another approach is to take the focus off yourself so you can think. Say something like, "Turn to your neighbor and..." A third tool, as we have emphasized, is the paraphrase, essential in all facilitation work. Paraphrase to let others know you've heard and want to understand. The paraphrase will often translate to others what was said. Come prepared, we've learned. Then be in the moment.

We've also been members of groups in which conditions are ideal and the facilitator moves the group efficiently through each agenda item to a final quick meeting assessment. Circumstances like this are not that rare, especially after a group has worked together for a while. But occasionally adjustment is still required.

Know that the substance of your work is you, not the planning.

TOOLS FOR FACILITATORS

To *prepare... don't attach* in regard to one's plans, facilitators choose tools that support flexibility.

WHAT: **Parking Lot**

WHY: Deflect a request for changing or adding a topic.

HOW: Should a member offer an idea unrelated to the current topic, the facilitator records the idea on a chart under the heading "Parking Lot" and says, "That's an important idea. Let's come back to it when we can give it full attention." Group members can add items to the Parking Lot using markers or sticky notes. To maintain trust, Parking Lot items do need to be addressed at some future time.

TIME:	GROUP SIZE:	MATERIALS:
Less than a minute	Any	Chart paper, sticky notes, markers

WHAT: **Applause**

WHY: Break rapport with subgroups and return to full group.

HOW: At the close of time for small-group work, ask participants to give themselves a hand. Model by clapping.

TIME:	GROUP SIZE:	MATERIALS:
Less than a minute	Any	None

WHAT: **Relevancy Check**

WHY: Maintain focus on current topic.

HOW: With an approachable voice (see p. 24) the facilitator says, "[Person's name], help us understand how your comment relates to the topic we're exploring." Speakers will either explain the relevance, in which case the conversation proceeds, or take it off the table.

TIME:	GROUP SIZE:	MATERIALS:
Less than a minute	Any	None

WHAT: **Airplane Stacking**

WHY: Members hear others' ideas because they're not worried about their place in a queue.

HOW: Explain the control-tower metaphor directing the order in which planes land. Assign numbers to those with raised hands, allowing them to lower their hands. Call on people in order.

TIME:	GROUP SIZE:	MATERIALS:
Less than a minute	Any	None

WHAT: **Visual Paragraph**

WHY: Aid clarity to multistep directions.

HOW: After the first direction, break eye contact, drop head, move to a new spot, look up, and give the next direction. In an approachable voice ask, "What questions about these directions do you have?"

TIME:	GROUP SIZE:	MATERIALS:
Less than a minute	Any	None

WHAT: **Acknowledge Resistance**

WHY: Proactively choreograph openings to potentially problematic meetings.

HOW: Facilitator uses verbal and nonverbal tools in these phases:

1. Connect with and welcome the audience, offer a charted agenda, then say, "Before we get started..."
2. Break eye contact, breathe, and move to another spot in the room. Reestablish eye contact and acknowledge any resistance by saying something like, "Some of you have disagreed with/had problems with some things we've discussed and don't want to be here."
3. Break eye contact, breathe, and move to another spot in the room. Reestablish eye contact and normalize and honor the group members' feelings, saying, "You're feeling this way because," for example, "time is tight and assessments are due."
4. Pause, then suggest the value of working together. "Given how much you value your students' well-being, you might be open to collectively explore options."
5. Finally, break and breathe again, move back to the original starting point at the agenda chart, and begin the first agenda item.

With thanks to Kendall Zoller.

TIME:	GROUP SIZE:	MATERIALS:
3–5 minutes	Any	Agenda chart, room to move

WHAT: **Topic as Given, Topic as Understood**

WHY: To check for understanding and group member readiness for a next topic.

HOW: With a *credible voice* (see p. 24), the facilitator names the next topic or task, with the information clearly displayed on a chart. Then define key words. Next the facilitator pauses, breaks eye contact, silently moves to a new space and in an *approachable voice* asks, "Just to be sure that I stated that clearly, what is the next topic (or task)?"

TIME:	GROUP SIZE:	MATERIALS:
2–3 minutes	Any	Charted agenda

WHAT: **Paraphrasing**

WHY: Offer a speaker's information back to them for reflection, clarification, and to check for understanding.

HOW: Paraphrases reflect a speaker's content and emotions and frame a level of abstraction for holding the content. The paraphrase reflects content back to the speaker for further consideration and connects the response to the flow of discourse emerging within the group.

There are broad uses of this tool. Paraphrasing within a flow of discourse often moves through a sequence of acknowledging, organizing, and abstracting. (Garmston & Wellman, 2016).

1. **Acknowledging** emotion and content. "So you're concerned about the budgeting process and ways to get input early." If the paraphrase is not completely accurate, the speaker will offer corrections.
2. **Organizing** themes and "containers" to group several statements or separate jumbled issues. This is an especially important type of paraphrase when multiple speakers contribute to a topic. "There appear to be two issues here. One is resource allocation and the other is the impact of those decisions on student learning."
3. **Abstracting.** Paraphrases move to a higher level of abstraction when they name concepts, goals, values and assumptions. "So a major goal here is to define fairness in the budgeting processes and compare those criteria to the operating values of the school."

TIME:	GROUP SIZE:	MATERIALS:
1 or 2 minutes (each time)	Any	None

PROCESSES FOR GROUPS

To *prepare... don't attach* to one's plans, facilitators choose processes that support flexibility.

WHAT: **Six-Step Response**

WHY: Respond to disruptive member and ensure psychological safety for group.

HOW: Practice following this pattern when a participant disrupts the group, for example with a loud complaint:

- Facilitator moves.
- Ask the person's name.
- Politely inquire about the person's issue.
- Paraphrase the response using the person's own intonation.
- Briefly converse as appropriate.
- Ask if the person is willing to wait for a break to have a conversation with the facilitator.

TIME:	GROUP SIZE:	MATERIALS:
1–3 minutes	Any	None

WHAT: **Mix-Freeze-Pair**

WHY: Energize and regroup.

HOW: Instruct members to stand and move around the room. At a signal, freeze and pair with the nearest person. Sit together and respond to a prompt.

TIME:	GROUP SIZE:	MATERIALS:
Less than a minute	Any	None

WHAT: **Elephant Walk**

WHY: Break tension and bring important topics into the light of day.

HOW: Explain the expression "the elephant in the room" as something large that everyone sees but are reluctant to acknowledge. Ask group members, "What are we not talking about that we should be?" Members record answers on index cards, then stand and collect more responses from other group members. (An alternative - "Elephant Talk" - is to ask group members to talk to their neighbor or small group.) When seated again, facilitator debriefs topics and gets a finger vote on each.

TIME:	GROUP SIZE:	MATERIALS:
7 minutes	Any	Index cards, pens

WHAT: **Fist to Five**

WHY: Quick read of the group's engagement and the relevance of the current topic/process.

HOW: Explain that a fist is the lowest rating, and five open fingers is the highest. Ask the group: "How engaged are you?" or "How valuable is this topic/process?" or "How likely is it you will follow through?

Facilitator notes and reports the data out loud to the group. For example "There are all 4's and 5's which means we can move this item forward."

TIME:	GROUP SIZE:	MATERIALS:
1–2 minutes	Any	None

WHAT: **Post-It Preferences**

WHY: Group makes decisions for itself about what's important.

HOW: Pose the question: "What topics are most important for this group?" Have group members write their ideas on sticky notes and stick them on a wall. Then make a graph, moving the sticky notes around based on topics.

TIME:	GROUP SIZE:	MATERIALS:
5–7 minutes	Any	Sticky notes, markers or pens, a clear wall

Reflecting

Take a moment by yourself or with a colleague to consider these questions.

1. Recall a time when you unexpectedly "pulled something from your back pocket" that perfectly fit the situation. What happened? What do you believe your "earlier self" might have learned?
2. From where has your best work emerged? What role did spontaneity play?
3. Consider ways this mindset's principles and strategies might also apply to teaching.

Try This

1. Initiate conversations with people you don't know well. This provides practice with spontaneity. Paraphrase what they say prior to adding your own thoughts.
2. Practice spontaneous responses. When a person asks you for how to handle a situation, say, "A story might shed some light." Pause and then tell them something from your reservoir of experiences.
3. Add these phrases to your repertoire in response to a question:
   - "Let's hear from others. Talk to your neighbor and prepare to report out." Or...
   - "What would be a goal in this situation?" Or...
   - "What criteria might you apply to this solution?"

Looking Back/Looking Ahead

When outcomes are as clear as the North Star, flexible facilitators have the greatest influence facilitating a group's growth and success. Spontaneous facilitators signal to the group that they are listening and in tune with the group's needs and particular dynamics in the moment. With a flexible mindset, facilitators are able to effectively respond to changes in the group's circumstances or unexpected problems and tasks in appropriate and creative ways. Flexibility allows a facilitator to be responsive to the group members' shifting perspectives and needs as well as to use emergent understandings and data to develop solutions. This disposition allows a facilitator to be receptive and responsive to diverse group perspectives, cultures, lenses, and mental models. Chapter 4 extends understandings about diversity, how it enriches groups, patterns for supporting it, and if needed, ways to intervene should aggressions occur. The inclusion of multiple perspectives is an important characteristic of effective groups.

Interlude

Diversity and conflict are the themes of the next two chapters, and each requires willingness to persevere though potentially difficult conversations and apply personal communication skills to maintain group cohesion and therefore achieve the best outcomes for students. Groups can and do acquire pragmatic knowledge on these topics and skills that allow them to understand one another and disagree agreeably. These chapters offer necessary knowledge about diversity and conflict in addition to effective facilitator tools and processes for groups.

Without capable conversations related to diversity and conflict, groups operate below their potential. Important perceptions and ideas are lost. Agreements become difficult to reach, and relationships are sometimes damaged. We have rarely observed or experienced effective conversation about diversity and conflict when a group lacks understanding and skills. Groups without an investment in these resources often experience emotionally charged conversations and collective frustration. Members become detached, others feel misunderstood, and still others might experience rejection. The binding fabric of effective group work deteriorates. Toxic qualities of disagreement may surge: passive aggressiveness, avoidance, competition or compromise. Meetings become more tense than collegial.

To engage and benefit from the Diversity Matters and Never Waste a Good Conflict mindsets, psychological safety and interpersonal communications skills are needed. Accomplished groups consider temporary conflict as an investment that sustains robust results in their work. Often, individuals don't feel safe enough or brave enough to speak their perceptions or truths. They may feel they are not skillful or will make matters worse by speaking. Without appropriate resources, member participation declines and constructive conversations are lost.

Teams that value group development build and hone resources for addressing conflict and diversity. Self-awareness is fundamental for both members and facilitator. Processes for hard-to-talk-about topics should be adopted, and interpersonal communication skills that allow frank expression without threat to differing perceptions should be practiced by all.

Learning to competently address each of these mindsets is an on-ramp for success.

CHAPTER 4
Diversity Enriches: *Inclusion Makes Groups Smarter*

Groups with a mix of perspectives, experiences, cultures, and job descriptions achieve substantially better results than more homogeneous groups.

The facilitator should create communication norms at the onset of the meeting. These norms should help to establish trust with all those in the meeting. Fairness and equal attention to all those present has a great impact on the success of a meeting.

—Grade 9 Teacher, California

I'd like to know how to guide the process of learning, collaborating and creating plans with a diverse group of people.

—Grade 3 Teacher & Literacy Coach, Ypsilanti, Michigan

As a facilitator a goal I have set for myself is to practice listening non-judgmentally to different points of view.

—Teacher-Leader/Data Coach, Los Angeles

Tensions Teachers Identified

- How to get ownership of shared mission, beliefs, values, and goals.
- How to support members who feel disempowered and inadequate.
- How to manage hidden agendas.
- How to bring together disagreeing folks.
- How to balance voice and participation of all members.
- How to develop groups with insufficient skills.
- How to enhance trust.
- How to make meetings meaningful for all.
- How to keep groups focused and motivated.

Diversity Enriches
Principles for This Mindset

1. Pay attention to self and others.
2. Teams with diverse membership include varied experiences and perspectives that are used to contribute to decisions with greater objectivity and effectiveness than homogeneous groups.
3. Well-functioning, diverse teams grow intellectually and socially in greater depth and more quickly.
4. Psychological safety is essential for direct, productive conversations.
5. Self-awareness is an essential resource.
6. Groups need various lenses and tools to harvest the resources of diversity.
7. The most effective groups are intentional about having conversations around the value of diversity and inclusion.
8. Views from diverse points of view are considered conceptual resources.
9. Homogeneous thinking produces bland results.

Relevant Information

A group of high school curriculum department heads are meeting to create a plan for improving the productiveness of their regular meetings during the coming year.

Frances, the group's facilitator, would like to provide the department heads with tools so they are more actively engaged and leave meetings feeling a sense of accomplishment. Frances holds an assumption that the greater the diversity of voices, the more productive the group can be.

Frances begins by sharing a public agenda. The first item is "Use today's meeting to gather data and develop understandings of our interactions." The group agrees to assign one group member to gather data by scripting the conversations during the meeting.

Data to be gathered:

Record indicators of engagement:

1. *who actively participates;*
2. *the nature of participation (the group's use of statements of inquiry, advocacy, and paraphrasing).*

The topic for dialogue is displayed on a chart: What might be ways to balance everyone's voice and participation in our meetings?

Frances suggests that the group move away from their computers and sit in a circle for the conversation, explaining that this allows members to better see each other, support a sense of belonging and encourage everyone to share. During the conversation Frances notices that Imani is quiet and inquires: "Imani, what are some of your thoughts or wonderings"? Imani smiles and shares, "Here are a few strategies that we used in my former district to improve our meetings." The dialogue continues for thirty minutes. Frances invites Round-Robin sharing and charting of ideas that are most useful for the group.

The group analyzes the data from their conversation. They notice patterns that affect group dynamics. Everyone shared at least once, there were mostly advocacy statements, only two questions, and paraphrases came from Frances. Two people of color were cut off several times, and the newest team member shared least. Two members were very active, while others made only a few comments.

At the end of the meeting, Frances asked the members to show a fist-to-five assessment of the usefulness of today's meeting. The members show fours and fives and express interest in setting a goal around facilitating an equitable and inclusive environment. They plan to examine which voices in particular are excluded and why, and what it might mean for the group to live the value of honoring diverse perspectives.

Diversity matters. Cement is durable and strong because of the variety of components used to create it. In human terms, strength in diversity is created by a collection of people representing a broad spectrum of demographics and philosophical differences. Teams that are aware of this and consciously invite varied perspectives are more likely to be safe havens for equitable, creative work.

There are infinite ways that humans are diverse, among them culture, race, religion, age, gender, sexual orientation, disability, socioeconomic foregrounds and backgrounds, education, capabilities, personality, worldviews, and philosophical perspectives. A diverse team brings many identities to the table.

Harvesting the resources of diversity requires recognition, inclusion, acceptance, and respect for individual differences and a variety of human uniqueness. More than this, harvesting diversity means that policies and group culture change. Groups may be diverse in many ways, both visibly and invisibly.

Group members must feel safe and comfortable enough to be themselves, voice their ideas, and feel they belong. Safety is grounded in group agreements; understandings of meanings for diversity, equity, and inclusion; knowing the benefits for individuals and the collective; and ways to honor and actualize these ideals in meetings.

The most productive group diversity is not just based on intelligence, racial, ethnic, or personality diversity, but on differences in life experiences and resulting deep cultural mental models. Culture is the way that every brain makes sense of the world, therefore, regardless of ethnicity or race, all people have a culture (Hammond, 2015).

> Deep culture is made up of tacit knowledge and unconscious assumptions that govern our world view. Two people from different deep cultures can look at the same event and have very different reactions to it because of the meaning they attach to the event based on their deep culture. For example, in Eastern culture, the color red means good luck, in Western culture red means danger. Elements at this (deep cultural) level have an intense emotional charge (Hammond, 2015).

When group members have different sets of assumptions, worldviews, and mental models, and the group possesses strategies for inclusive engagement, decision-making is less likely to get mired and more likely to result in flexible and innovative solutions. When group members are too similar, the group is not high-performing because it is susceptible to groupthink: "that inability to hear different voices and perspectives" (Garmston & von Frank, 2012).

In *Culturally Proficient Coaching: Supporting Educators to Create Equitable Schools,* the authors describe an educator with cultural competency as one who commits to the elimination of human-made barriers to student learning achievement (Lindsey et al., 2020.) How do educators develop consistent practices to eliminate such barriers? The challenge is to facilitate group meetings where we consciously use strategies and conversation structures to facilitate fairness, impartiality, and balance.

In the scenario above, Frances's goal was to support the group in moving toward equity and inclusion. She did it a) using principles, tools, and structures; b) clearly stating purpose; c) raising the issue of inclusion; d) using a talking circle; e) posting visuals such as agenda, questions, and brainstormed ideas; f) inviting engagement by facilitating Round-Robin sharing; g) employing a group-member meeting assessment; and (h) facilitating data-driven goal setting. When principles and practices such as these become routine, the result is multicultural and multi-perspective teams that are wellsprings of creativity and innovation that collaboratively make decisions with greater effectiveness and shelf life.

What Facilitators Need to Know

Facilitator self-awareness is a foundation to competent work. As expressed by the seminal wisdom of philosopher Kahlil Gibran: Knowledge of the self is the mother of all knowledge.

Facilitators have high consciousness of their lenses and filters and the impact that these have on their mental models, perceptions, and behavioral choices. Facilitators are intentionally nonjudgmental, able to notice internal tensions, and willing to set aside personal opinions that may hinder being open to all voices and points of view. They manage the polarities of paying attention to self while paying attention to others, maintaining both macro and micro views, and being simultaneously aware of happenings in the external environment while observing their internal states.

All five of the mindsets presented in this book work synergistically. Facilitators are encouraged to review them together and reflect on how each supports a holistic approach to facilitation.

Assuming that others' intentions are not meant to be harmful shows respect for others and encourages open, honest conversations about difficult and important topics (Garmston & Wellman, 2016). Presuming positive intent also supports facilitator goodwill through language, framing questions, ideas, and paraphrases in ways to reduce members perceiving threats or challenges. Statements like these help: "Given our shared concern for balanced participation, what might be some best ways to structure our meetings?" or "Here are the data we generated. What stands out as most important?" or "Felicia, you are reminding us of the importance of seeking all stakeholder opinions."

What stories are you telling yourself about a person, group, or situation? While facilitating a fourth grade team meeting, Phil noticed Hasan frowning and looking towards the ceiling. Phil's stomach tightened as he silently said to himself, *There he goes again. Hasan is always planning a critical comment that derails the group!* Berger (2019) cautions leaders about the seduction of a "simple story." She calls this habit a "leadership mind trap," stating that our desire for a simple story can blind us to reality.

Stories have been sources of meaning, connection, survival, and comfort for humans. The good news is that we are now perfectly wired for stories; the bad news is that our automatic stories are probably too simple for a complex world. Our brains have developed to create patterns of beginning, middle and end (Berger, 2019).

Berger states that when this pattern is not satisfying for us, we feel stressed, and we fill in the missing pieces with our own narrative. She offers keys to unlock our simple stories. One suggestion is to always have multiple stories about people and life events and to ask, "How is this person a hero?" For example, Phil could ask himself, "How might Hasan's ideas propel the group towards better decisions?" Phil could tell himself that Hasan has unique perspectives to open the group to unseen possibilities. He could frame the meeting as an adventure for discovering new territories or for forging new relationships. As facilitator, ask yourself, "How might this situation be different if I tell myself a different story?" Phil could also become curious and ask Hasan, "What wonderings are you having about our topic?"

Facilitators are models and catalysts for productive attitudes, mindsets, capabilities, and behaviors. They craft safe social-cognitive-emotional containers by living the norms, listening to understand, paraphrasing, normalizing and naming tensions, promoting a spirit of inquiry, inviting differing perspectives, and giving the what, why, how of information and processes.

Three types of facilitator paraphrases are particularly useful when navigating diverse perspectives. One is the *common-ground paraphrase*. This statement organizes and unifies different opinions, interests or ideas. An example: "While there are various ideas about student conduct, you all value the goal of promoting student self-management."

A second type is the *polarity paraphrase* which normalizes tensions and integrates seemingly competing values. An example: "You're wondering how to honor students' efforts while challenging them to grow." The common-ground and polarity paraphrases are two examples of the

Abstracting Paraphrase, introduced in Chapter 3.

In a third type, facilitators *acknowledge emotions* without diminishing resourcefulness. An example: "We are feeling overwhelmed because we want to meet the needs of all students."

Facilitating inclusive meetings is a courageous act. Know that you are enough! Know that you can learn from experiences and do make a difference. Efficacy is the greatest predictor of success.

What Groups Need to Know

Establishing norms that will govern the group's work towards inviting multiple voices into meetings is crucial. To create norms, teams must agree to the importance of having conversations about diversity, diverse perspectives, and equity of voice. Yet issues of equity, inclusion, race, gender, sexuality, class, language, and culture remain difficult topics for teams to raise and talk about. "Educators at all levels need to develop the courage, knowledge, dispositions, and skills to understand the racial realities and cultural considerations brought about by demographic changes in US schools" (Howard et al., 2019, p.1).

In high-performing groups, members are clear about what diversity means to them. They value it and seek it out when it's missing. Inclusivity requires creating conditions in which members feel psychologically safe. Psychological safety contributes to the full engagement of members of any group. Harvard Business School Professor Amy Edmondson, in her book *The Fearless Organization: Creating Psychological Safety in the Workplace for Learning, Innovation, and Growth,* states that psychological safety is a belief that one will not be punished or humiliated for speaking up with ideas, questions, concerns, or mistakes. She asserts that psychological safety is important and it takes work, but it's worth the effort (2019). In meetings, who contributes, how contributions are treated, and the ways in which we engage with our colleagues all matters. The effort it takes to reimagine norms is worth the energy and time spent.

Setting the groundwork for developing new agreements for creating equity and inclusion within meetings is crucial, but without practice and intentionality, the group may remain stuck in old habits, unconscious to bias, and slip back into existing operating patterns. Safe spaces aren't always comfortable spaces. Group members must be brave enough to hang out in some discomfort. Arao and Clemens (2013) advocate that we shift from the terminology of *safe space* to *brave space,* to support members in normalizing and expecting tensions.

Listening to understand and its outward manifestation as paraphrasing are essential for inclusive dialogue. One of the most useful responses a group member can give another expresses an attempt to understand what really matters to that person and their values. "*So what's important to you,* Aziz, is that we consider the impact of our actions on others." Building trusting relationships where all members feel valued and authentically heard requires skill in the structures and tools of dialogue: turn taking, pausing, paraphrasing, and posing psychologically safe questions (Garmston and Wellman, 2016).

MICROAGGRESSIONS

Culturally savvy groups are aware of microaggressions. Groups that lack the consciousness, willingness, and ability to converse and strategize around equity and inclusion end up fostering implicit and unconscious bias. These biases are typically activated involuntarily, usually without awareness or intentional control. They impact our understanding, actions, and decisions in an unconscious manner (Rudd, 2014). This unconsciousness can surface as microaggressions.

Microaggressions are day-to-day, often unintentional but harmful interactions against a person from a marginalized group. While microaggressions are not as intense in tone or tenor as harassment or discrimination, these interactions leave the recipients feeling uncomfortable or insulted. Microaggressions are the externalization of people's biases toward marginalized groups. They are the daily verbal, nonverbal, and environmental slights, brushoffs, or disrespectful comments—deliberate or accidental—which convey threatening, pejorative, or damaging messages to people predicated exclusively upon the fact that they belong to a disenfranchised group (Wing Sue, 2010).

A department lead compliments an Asian American woman for speaking perfect English. English is her first language.

Tina, an African American group member, passionately offers an idea she is excited about and is asked, "Why are you so angry?"

Joseph, who uses a wheelchair, is greeted by the meeting facilitator with, "Hey, if you can get here early, why can't the others? You're an inspiration!"

Kristal speaks up in a meeting, but she can barely get her words out because of being continuously interrupted by her male team members.

What distinguishes microaggressions from other rude or unkind expressions is their connection to a person's membership in a group that is discriminated against or is the subject of societal stereotypes. In this sense, microaggressions are closely related to implicit biases, which are attitudes, stereotypes, and assumptions we hold and are not aware of, and that impact our thoughts and behaviors.

When microaggression comments, questions, or actions happen in meetings, most often the recipient squirms, winces internally, and says nothing, not knowing how to respond for a variety of reasons. Group members may feel awkward and uncomfortable if they have little experience responding appropriately. Some group members may feel they will jeopardize their status and sense of belonging if they come to the aid of the victim (Khanna, 2019).

Microaggressions break relationships and make it more difficult to develop the trust and vulnerability needed for teamwork. In the speaker's view, a microaggression statement is often made with good intention, as a compliment or a way of acknowledging the recipient's intelligence or contributions to the team. Despite these good intentions, such remarks can still hurt. And when microaggressions happen repeatedly to someone, the resulting stress can lead to poor health and low job satisfaction (Khanna, 2019).

Developing consciousness about and responding to microaggressions requires intentionality. Abrams, in her work about having tough conversations, cites a variety of reflection questions and suggestions to support self-awareness and taking action as a witness to microaggressions:

- Realize the "nice" thing to do is to speak up.
- Realize that anything other than civil and respectful dialogue is unacceptable. Focus on that point in order to remain calm as you express that expectation.
- Ask yourself, "Is there a way that I could tell my truth and manage my communication so that however defensive the person could become, he or she would be less likely to take out that anger on others?"

- Ask yourself, "How valuable is my personal comfort compared with the effort I would have to make to result in long-term gains for others?"
- Ask yourself, "Who am I/we protecting?"
- Ask yourself, "How might this be affecting student learning?"

Additional recommendations for group members to avoid perpetrating microaggressions on colleagues include: 1) be constantly vigilant of your own biases and fears; 2) seek out interactions with people who differ from you; and 3) be open to discussing your own attitudes and biases and how they might have hurt others (Khanna, 2019).

TOOLS FOR FACILITATORS

Because *diversity enriches,* facilitators choose tools that support inclusion.

WHAT: **Procedure Check**

WHY: Include all voices and encourage fairness.

HOW: Invite group members to participate in decision-making regarding agenda items, organizational structures, methods of participating (see Group Choice, Chapter 3).

TIME:	GROUP SIZE:	MATERIALS:
2–5 minutes	Any	Chart paper, markers or whiteboard

WHAT: **Assumptions Inquiry**

WHY: Identify and clarify individual or group assumptions.

HOW:

1. Invite members to list their assumptions related to a challenge or initiative. Assumptions related to professional development, for example, might include:
   - limited time available,
   - must take place in seminar settings,
   - some teachers are resistant.
2. Invite the group to inquire about these assumptions:
   - What data inform them?
   - What might be alternative interpretations to the same data?
   - In which aspects are the assumptions generalizable, and in which aspects are they situational?

TIME:	GROUP SIZE:	MATERIALS:
6–10 minutes	Any	Chart paper, markers, whiteboard or chalkboard

WHAT: **Pause, Paraphrase, Pose a Question Pattern**

WHY: Establish a normative pattern of respectful listening and inquiry.

HOW: Model, teach, and monitor 3 to 5 seconds of wait time and uninterrupted listening, followed by checking for understanding through the use of paraphrase (see Paraphrasing, Chapter 3). Getting "sign off" on a paraphrase gives permission to pose a question.

TIME:	GROUP SIZE:	MATERIALS:
1–3 minutes	Any	None

WHAT: **Small Fires**

WHY: Remove physical barriers and distractions to conversation.

HOW: Move team members away from tables and form a circle of chairs. Remove any empty chairs, so there are no gaps. Leave laptops, phones, and other distractions behind so group members are encouraged to be fully present with one another.

Tip: Use for Grounding (see Grounding on p. 68), dialogue, and inclusion.

TIME:	GROUP SIZE:	MATERIALS:
5 minutes for setup	Rearrange into groups of 4-8	Open space to form circles, chairs

WHAT: **Balance Participation**

WHY: Gain the enrichment of diverse voices while respectfully including all group members.

HOW: Facilitators balance participation by doing the following:

- Make an overt standard for all meetings, establishing balance as a procedural norm;
- Invite participation by all through inclusive language, and calling on people who have not yet contributed. (Recall the opening of this chapter when Frances noticed that Imani is quiet and inquires: "Imani, what are some of your thoughts or wonderings?")
- Structure for balance through interactive processing strategies—from a simple "Turn to your neighbor and share..." to the group processes offered in this book (see Inclusion Strategies on p. 67).

TIME:	GROUP SIZE:	MATERIALS:
As often as possible	Any	None

PROCESSES FOR GROUPS

Because *diversity enriches,* facilitators choose processes that support contributions from diverse perspectives. Inclusion strategies support getting all voices heard nonjudgmentally early on in a meeting, surface personal agendas in a nonconfrontational way, and build community. Some examples are *I'm In* (Chapter 1), *Prioritizing Outcomes* (Chapter 2), *Inter-Venn-tion* (see Inter-Venn-tion below), and *Grounding* (see Grounding on p. 68).

WHAT: **Inter-Venn-tion**

WHY: Provide introductions in a newly formed group to connect group members.

HOW: Guide members through these steps:

- Get into pairs.
- Draw a large Venn diagram (two circles with some overlap) on paper, and write partner names in each circle.
- Engage in conversation, writing items of common ground in the overlapping part of the Venn, and write differences on the outer part of the Venn circles.
- Pairs use the Venn diagram to introduce their partner to the full group, or to another pair or sub-group (Lipton & Wellman, 2011).

Tip: For uneven groups, use some trios/triple Venn.

TIME:	GROUP SIZE:	MATERIALS:
5–7 minutes	4+	Paper, markers, whiteboard or chalkboard

WHAT: **Grounding**

WHY: A tightly structured protocol allows for equity of voice, turn-taking, free expression, and members being heard.

HOW: Explain the procedure.

- Members take turns talking. For large groups, break into subgroups.
- When one member talks, all others are silent.
- Full nonverbal attention is given to the speaker.
- After everyone has talked, the first speaker summarizes what was said.
- Post what members should talk about.
    - My name is...
    - My relationship to this topic is...
    - My expectations are...
    - How I feel about being here is...

When members indicate that they understand the process, the facilitator asks the first speaker(s), notified in advance, to begin. When the group (or all groups) are finished, report out themes to the full group.

TIME:	GROUP SIZE:	MATERIALS:
15–25 minutes	Rearrange into groups of 4-6	Space to form "small fires," a circles of chairs for each group

WHAT: **Data-Driven Dialogue**

WHY: Provide a process for analyzing data that is respectful, thoughtful, and creates a shared meaning of data.

HOW: Data-Driven Dialogue (Wellman & Lipton, 2017) is a structured process that involves three phases.

- **Activating & Engaging** – Surfacing experiences, possibilities, expectations, and predicting what the data will indicate. A potential facilitator prompt might be: "What predications might you make about what these data will indicate?"
- **Exploring & Discovering** – Analyzing the data. A potential facilitator prompt might be: "In what ways do the data compare to your predictions?"
- **Organizing & Integrating** – Generating theory, inferring why the data are what they are and identifying questions that might require further investigation. A potential facilitator prompt might be: "Based on your analysis, what additional data might be helpful?"

TIME:	GROUP SIZE:	MATERIALS:
30–45 minutes	Rearrange into groups of 4-6	Visuals of the data, chart paper, markers

WHAT: **People and Principles**

WHY: Group creation and ownership of principles to guide inclusive and respectful behavioral choices and promote safe and brave diversity conversations.

HOW:

1. Facilitator displays images of a wide variety of diversity in human systems, such as various family structures, work and play groups, teams, religious groups, gender identities, disabilities, ages, jobs, race, culture, ethnicity, economic statuses, etc. Pictures should also show people engaged in a variety of activities.
2. Group members examine the images and reflect on this question: "What might be some universal truths about all social systems?"
3. Facilitator engages group in *brainstorm charting* of the universal truths.
4. Facilitator shares these statements visually:
    a. *Universal truths can become principles for how we interact with others.*
    b. *Principles guide our behavioral choices.*
5. Facilitator offers one example of each:
    a. Universal truth: *The actions of one person impact the entire system.*
    b. Principle: *Pay attention to both myself and others.* Or *Choose my actions wisely.*
6. Facilitator gives directions visually:
   Considering these universal truths you brainstormed [point to chart], *how might these translate into principles that might guide our behavior?*
7. Chart principles.

8. Facilitate a conversation that includes,
    a. *What are some ways these principles might support equity and inclusion in our meetings?*
    b. *How might we keep these principles at the forefront or our mindsets and behaviors?*

TIME:	GROUP SIZE:	MATERIALS:
30 minutes	3+	Images of diverse groups, chart paper or white board, markers

Reflecting

Take a moment by yourself or with a colleague to consider these questions:

1. What do you notice about your developing comfort with pausing first, checking for understanding with a paraphrase, and following up with a question that further opens thinking?
2. What are some of the ways you are finding to acknowledge and build on diversity in your meetings?
3. As you review the strategies presented in this book, what do you notice about how they support you with balancing participation? How might you continue to balance participation in your meetings?

Try This

1. Construct your own list of inclusion strategies, and add to it periodically. (See *The Adaptive School: A Sourcebook for Developing Collaborative Groups* for ideas, and visit www.thinkingcollaborative.com/as-resources, "Strategies and Moves.")
2. Review *What Facilitators Need to Know* in this chapter, and prioritize the top three important points for you. Create an action plan with resources and support to stretch yourself in those three areas. Include a celebration of your accomplishments in your plan.

Looking Back/Looking Ahead

Systems that are the most diverse are the most adaptive. The most productive teams are those that value and use the resources of diverse perspectives. Valuing diversity means seeking diverse viewpoints, exploring options from varied perspectives, seeking to understand others, respecting minority positions, and honoring different ways of thinking.

The first step in facilitating inclusive group meetings is to establish norms that will govern the group's work towards inviting multiple voices into meetings. To create norms, teams must agree to the importance of having conversations about diversity, diverse perspectives, and equity of voice. In high-performing groups members are clear about what diversity means. They value it and seek its inclusion when it's missing. Inclusivity requires creating conditions in which members feel psychologically safe.

Facilitators introduce practices that enable equity of voice and respectfully balanced participation. It is important for facilitators to understand that diversity is always present in groups, and differences create environments where conflict is inevitable. Chapter 5 explores how tensions can become a source of productive energy and group learning.

CHAPTER 5
Never Let a Conflict Go to Waste: *Liberate Opportunities*

> Crisis is an opportunity to do things you think you couldn't do before.

Toxic teams and people who aren't on the same page and feel no control over outcomes.

—Instructional Coach, Michigan

How do you build consensus among the meeting participants? A major challenge is that teachers do not know the outcomes for which they are looking.

—Director of Teaching and Learning, Chennai, India

How do you make decisions that everyone can live with and not sabotage?

—Middle School Teacher, Midwestern United States

Tensions Teachers Identified

- How do I deal with teachers who negatively influence others?
- How do I get everyone to have a common focus or vision of best practices?
- What are some ways to refocus negativity?
- What strategies ensure everyone is valued?
- How do I remain in a facilitator role when others want me to be an active participant?
- What can I do to keep the group safe?
- How do I address conflict directed at me as facilitator?

Never Let A Conflict Go To Waste
Principles for This Mindset

1. Conflict is inevitable and until it's addressed it becomes increasingly difficult to work with.
2. For conflict to be productive, participants must know they are heard.
3. Groups without conflict tend toward apathy.
4. Knowledge about ways to approach conflict and practicing interpersonal skills positively influence morale, efficacy, and goal attainment.
5. Engaging in conflict about ideas while minimizing interpersonal conflict produces quality decisions likely to satisfy all members.
6. Group members' capacity for graceful fighting is more important than facilitator skill.
7. Conflict about ideas (cognitive conflict) enriches quality of choices and decisions in groups.
8. Group working agreements are scaffolds for constructive conflict about ideas.
9. Teaching groups ways of addressing conflict generates high interest.

Relevant Information

Just as each cloud may have a silver lining, conflict can bring attention to existing issues hidden in plain view. Covid-19 led to major disruptions in schooling. The ways we devised to keep students safe yet still learning exposed lurking, unseen issues. Educators, but also the country at large, learned the magnitude of unequal access to learning in US schools. Parents marveled at what teachers do when they were enlisted to teach their own children. New challenges emerged for teachers working online without the usual connections with students.

Facilitators with the Never Let a Conflict Go to Waste mindset presume that conflict may bring gifts. They know that disturbing a group into seeing unintended consequences can illuminate existing but untended problems. This is not comfortable. But as we've said earlier, uncomfortable topics can be addressed in ways that provide safety for members. As in much personal learning, some discomfort may be required. Every conflict in a department or grade-level team is a potential problem-solving opportunity in which students are winners.

Collectively the five mindsets described in this book form an integrated whole, a worldview of effective facilitation. Perceptive facilitators see groups as they could be and see conflict management as learnable. Aikido master Thomas Crum notes that being willing to change allows you to move from a point of view to a viewing point—a higher, more expansive place, a macrocentric view from which you can see multiple perspectives. People in this place know the unexpected can be expected, so they plan well yet prepare to improvise. They are clear that diversity is a benefit, not a disadvantage. And they discern that any group conflict can be used as a launching pad to learn more about teaching, learning, students, and themselves.

For groups to effectively work on task-related issues, they must have the skills to maintain their effectiveness when conflict between people appears, because it will. Throughout this book, interpersonal skills that are useful when emotions are high have been introduced. In Chapter 1 are reminders about being centered, conscious use of vocal patterns, and using positive presuppositions. The paraphrase was introduced in Chapter 3 and reappeared in other chapters. This is because the paraphrase is not only the most effective facilitator tool but is also the foundation of clear and respectful communication among team members.

Chapter 3 provided information on facilitation and ways facilitators can work most effectively with groups. Chapter 4 gave ideas and tools for working with diversity. Differences in cognitive style, region in a country of origin, ethnicity, gender, language, age, and other dimensions reappear continuously with those we encounter. And finally, this chapter provides additional tools and structures for working and living with conflict.

From discomfort comes the space and energy for positive change. However, it is not unusual to perceive conflict as threat. When emotions run high, people work to defend their interests. When something feels like an attack, it can spark antagonistic cycles of communication. Step back. Consider the other party's perspectives. This reframes the entire conflict and can provide a pathway to resolution. Listen to what is said and listen to what might be behind what is said. "The number one goal in resolving a conflict is to make sure both sides maintain their self-esteem. Resolving conflict is rarely about who is right. It is about acknowledgment and appreciation of differences" (Crum, 2021).

Listen for values, not issues. Teacher negotiations, for example, are often about salaries and benefits. Yet if teachers were asked what they value most, they might say respect, acknowledgment, and being valued. Salaries, in part, are tokens for being valued. Focus on what you want to achieve rather than on problems. When complaints are heard about the status quo ask what is wanted. Remember that people aren't against you, they are taking care of themselves.

Keep the conversation to one timeframe. Often comments in the same conversation can be about the past (why this became a problem), the future (what is hoped for), and the present (current behaviors that are keeping us stuck). Spend as little time in the past as possible. Even when everyone experienced the same event, individuals hold different memories. The past is useful only inasmuch as it illuminates what is wanted instead. We've found it useful to post a "Desired State Map" in the faculty room or some other setting where groups meet (see Tools for Facilitators on p. 81). The map is used to direct conversations from undesirable existing states to ones that are desired, identifying the resources necessary to get there. Again, talk in one temporal category at a time.

Keep it safe. Psychological safety is the most essential resource for group effectiveness in the normal course of business. During periods of disagreement and strife, it is even more necessary. Choose "tight" (highly scaffolded) processes for group conversations. Tight processes provide safety. Examples are offered in the Facilitator Tools and Processes for Groups later in this chapter.

One complication of reaching resolution in groups is that members most likely hold differing approaches to conflict. Everyone learned their approach first as a member of the most important group of their life, their family. Varying responses to conflict will be found within any faculty. For some, a default style is collaboration. Competition will be the go-to for others. Some avoid it. Others accommodate by making room in a proposal for others' ideas. Efforts to compromise may appear. If this is not yet complicated enough, add passive-aggressiveness and aggression to the mix. Each is employed to take care of oneself related to the discord of the moment. When two or more of these happen in the same dispute, arriving at resolution can be arduous, time consuming, and might achieve less-than-optimal results.

What Facilitators Need to Know

Facilitators help group members be heard and have their opinions valued by offering a common approach and guiding the group to work within its parameters. Groups do learn new understandings and skills about conflict when they work together toward common goals, when safe group processes are employed, and when they share a growth mindset.

Seek specificity whenever you hear "always" or "never." It's never never, but only a portion of it. Ask, "When you say 'never,' please give an example..." or "Is there ever a time..." When caught in a cycle of negativity, focus on what is wanted. Ask for the desired state.

Expect some challenges when helping a group become more conflict capable. In order to become more conversant in conflict situations, already scarce time must be used to acquire relevant concepts or to practice essential skills. Setting aside time for this work may be resisted, as groups already have too little time to work on current propositions.

Keep in mind that human conflict is largely a matter of differing perceptions, none of which hold the entire truth of a matter. People do the best they can with what they have. Efforts may be clumsy, but are usually driven by positive intentions. When a member makes an effort to compete but the group is attempting to collaborate, remove judgment and give the person a break. Remember that behaviors are attempts to take care of oneself.

Essential resources are needed to work with the currents of conflict. They include the ability to listen for understanding, to use language that connects rather than disrupts, and to keep the group on one topic at a time or one process at a time to protect people from attack. Add the tools and group processes described later in this chapter and others easily found elsewhere. Two of these resources are *The Adaptive School: A Sourcebook for Developing Collaborative Groups* (Garmston & Wellman 2016) and *Lemons to Lemonade* (Garmston & Zimmerman, 2013).

"Paraphrase your butt off!" is what Carolyn advises her mentees. Unless people feel heard, progress is halted. Listening to understand is simply explaining what you believe others to mean. We listen with our ears, of course, but also with our eyes, emotions, and intellect. Because listening is the single most important skill for a facilitator, we've addressed its use in each previous mindset. It is also basic to productive talk and conflict among group members. Facilitators and group members paraphrase frequently. Examples and reasons for paraphrasing appear in Tools for Facilitators, Chapter 3.

Support groups as they normalize tensions and polarities. Use and elaborate on language such as *natural tensions, engaging cognitive conflict, both/and thinking, diverse beliefs, and differing viewpoints.* Reframing tensions in this way supports viewing them as opportunities for enhancing group resourcefulness. Polarities are unavoidable and unsolvable but are perceived as chronic conflicts between people. "If the polarization is over a polarity, not only are both sides 'right,' they both need each other's wisdom to be successful over time" (Johnson, 2020, p. 7). Collaboratively creating a picture of the tension—a polarity map—helps groups to honor and expand perspectives, learn from conflict, and strategize positive results. Polarity Mapping is explored on p. 89 in Processes for Groups.

Use and teach strategic language when tension exists. The following examples were described in *Lemons to Lemonade* (2013) and drawn from the experiences of Diane Zimmerman and Bob Garmston.

- Take the focus off of yourself. Rather than saying, "I would like you to..." say, "Please pause and turn so you can see and hear one another," or "Please turn toward the chart that lists your agreements."
- Use descriptive words (someone is having a side conversation) rather than judgmental ones (someone is being rude). Give examples of what can be seen or heard. Say, "Priya decided to

include the data from last year," rather than "It was decided to...." The latter leaves an open question...who is deciding?

- Convert concepts into behaviors when problem solving. Conversations that attempt to solve problems by focusing on concepts are doomed. Respond to "They are not respecting us" by asking, "What might you see and hear when they are showing you respect?" or "What would they be doing if they were respecting you?"

What Groups Need to Know

> We learn more from people who challenge our thought processes than those who affirm our conclusions. Strong leaders engage their critics and make themselves stronger (Grant, 2021).

It's useful for groups to recognize two common types of conflict—cognitive and affective. One is productive, the other destructive. Cognitive conflicts, as described by Garmston & Wellman (2009), are productive disagreements about ideas. Interpersonal or affective conflict is disruptive. As long as disagreements among team members maintain a focus on substantive, issue-related differences of opinion, they tend to improve team effectiveness. Such cognitive conflict is a natural part of a properly functioning team. Cognitive conflict occurs as team members examine, compare, and reconcile differences. It requires teams to engage in activities that are essential to its effectiveness. Among these are gathering and analyzing data and selecting and developing essential skills like paraphrasing, asking open-ended questions, and being silent as others talk. It focuses attention on the all-too-often ignored assumptions that may underlie any particular issue.

Interpersonal conflict lowers team effectiveness by fostering hostility, distrust, cynicism, avoidance and apathy among team members. This type of conflict focuses on personalized anger or resentment usually directed at specific individuals rather than ideas. It often emerges when task completion becomes corrupted because members lack the skills or norms to disagree gracefully. In such settings, disagreement about ideas can become attacks towards an individual.

Whenever a group slides toward interpersonal conflict, reminders to get back on track must occur. It's important that group members make these interventions as well as the facilitator, because the group belongs to the group. When members exert leadership to improve group processes, collective resilience is a byproduct.

TOOLS FOR FACILITATORS

In order to *never let a conflict go to waste,* facilitators choose tools that help the group engage in cognitive conflict while minimizing affective conflict.

WHAT: **Set Working Agreements**

WHY: Maintain effectiveness, efficiency, and productive conflict.

HOW: Ask the group to suggest working guidelines for their meetings. These are behavioral guidelines. Ask the group to suggest agreements for ways they want their meetings to function. Brainstorm and make a list. Ask which are essential. Once 5 to 7 are identified, post them for that meeting, post them for future meetings, and include them on agendas. Members or the facilitator can remind someone when an agreement is not being used.

TIME:	GROUP SIZE:	MATERIALS:
10 minutes	Any	Chart paper, markers

WHAT: **Sufficient Consensus**

WHY: Simplify decision-making.

HOW: Through a discussion, agree on a suggested figure to represent consensus (such as 80%).

TIME:	GROUP SIZE:	MATERIALS:
10 minutes	Any	Flip chart

WHAT: **Stems of Connection**

WHY: Use language that connects people rather than divides them.

HOW: Model, teach, and monitor the following:

1. *And*, not *but*. When we respond to something, we often introduce our point with the word *but*. Create a pattern of saying *and* rather than *but*. *And* connects your idea with the previous person's thought while *but* refutes it and generates unnecessary tension and argument.
2. *I see it a different way*. Suggest this phrase as a means to introduce other points of view. It is valuable because it too eliminates unnecessary tension.
3. Agree to speak about the future rather than the past.
4. Agree on criteria for acceptable solutions before generating possible solutions.

TIME:	GROUP SIZE:	MATERIALS:
As often as appropriate	Any	None

WHAT: **Centi-Cents**

WHY: Simplify decision-making.

HOW: Members have one hundred imaginary pennies they can distribute across a few options to make a group decision. Present the options. Individuals decide how many pennies they will spend on each option. Gather and present the data to the group.

TIME:	GROUP SIZE:	MATERIALS:
8 minutes	Any	Handout with written options

WHAT: **Freeing Stuck Groups**

WHY: Resolving roadblocks.

HOW: The facilitator asks, "What's stopping us from making a decision?" or "Who would be willing to meet with [name] and [name] to develop a proposal for the next meeting?" or "Are you willing to give the subcommittee the authority to make that decision?" or "Would it be agreeable to the group if we asked [name] to bring us more information before we proceed?" or "I think this is a decision for [name]. Shall we ask her to make it?"

TIME:	GROUP SIZE:	MATERIALS:
4 minutes	Any	None

WHAT: **Relevancy Check**

WHY: Set aside off-topic comments.

HOW: A group member says something unrelated to the group's topic. With an approachable voice, the facilitator says, "[Name], help us understand how your comment relates to the topic we're exploring?" Speakers will either explain the relevance, in which case the conversation proceeds, or take it off the table. A variation is that the facilitator records the item on chart paper, announcing the group will return to it at an appropriate time.

NOTE: This strategy also appears in Chapter 2. It is repeated here because it functions to navigate group tensions.

TIME:	GROUP SIZE:	MATERIALS:
2 minutes	Any	Chart paper

WHAT: **Disagreement Grid**

WHY: Disagree agreeably.

HOW: Invite group members to participate as a warm-up for a conversation in which diverse opinions are held.

- Draw a four-by-four grid on a chart. Ask participants to assume that each square is equal in dimension to the other squares.
- Ask participants how many squares they see.
- As each number is offered, write it on the chart margin without comment.
- After several numbers are recorded, stop. Ask, "Who saw [one of the higher numbers] squares? Would you please explain to the group where you see these squares?"
- Mark on the grid as a member explains what they see.
- Ask: "Is the person who said sixteen wrong? Seventeen? Twenty-four?"
- Say, "As we move into our next conversation, a suggestion is that when you have a difference of opinion you say, 'I see it a different way.'"

TIME:	GROUP SIZE:	MATERIALS:
5 minutes	Any	Chart paper

WHAT: **Resolution Engagement**

WHY: Relieve tension with orderly process.

HOW: Focus on what members agree on, for instance by posting the mission, vision, and/or values statements to remind people why they are there.

- Ask members, "If this disagreement continues, where will we be? How will it hurt our organization?"
- Have members restate their position. If it will take longer than three minutes, allow opportunities for others to confirm or question for understanding (not disagreement).
- Shift to prioritizing alternatives, rather than excluding all alternatives but one.
- Take a 10-minute break in which each member quietly reflects on what he/she can do to move the group forward.
- Take 5 to 10 minutes and in pairs, ask each person to share what he/she is confused or irritated about. One person in the pair helps the other to articulate their views to the larger group. Then switch roles and repeat the process.
- Propose an "agree to disagree" disposition.
- If disagreement or lack of consensus persists around an issue, ask a subgroup to select options and report back to the full group.
- Call for a vote on a stated question or decision.

TIME:	GROUP SIZE:	MATERIALS:
30–40 minutes	Any	None

WHAT: **Desired State Map**

WHY: Reduce decision complexity and switch the timeframe to a future focus.

HOW: Display a desired-state map, as shown below.

- Explain that defining a desired state establishes a goal and is more important than exploring why the problem exists.
- The group names a desired state in broad terms.
- Next, develop a behavioral description. What would one see and hear when the desired state is achieved?
- Next identify the resources required to achieve the desired state.

Consider skills, knowledge, and behavior.

- Select the most catalytic of resources and develop a plan for creating them.

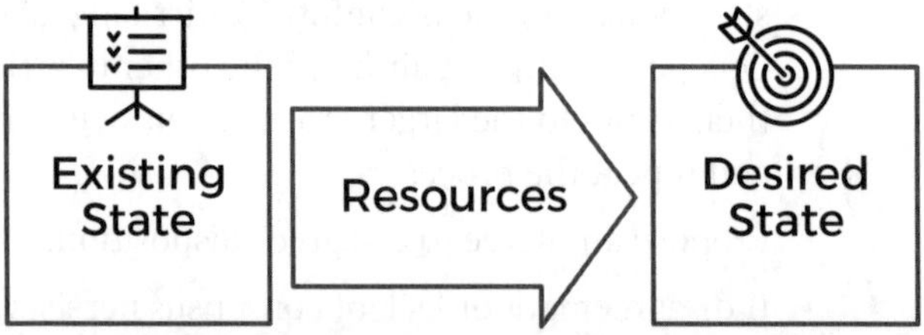

TIME:	GROUP SIZE:	MATERIALS:
20-35 minutes	2-12	Chart paper, markers

PROCESSES FOR GROUPS

To *never let a conflict go to waste* facilitators choose processes that help a group engage in cognitive conflict while minimizing affective conflict.

WHAT: **Assumptions Wall**

WHY: Bring cognitive conflict to light in a process that is emotionally safe.

HOW: Guide members through these steps.

- Individuals list assumptions about a topic.
- Have participants choose one that most informs their behavior.
- Participants write their choice on sentence strip in 8 to 12 words.
- Post assumptions on the wall.
- Facilitator models inquiry (approachable voice, plurals, invitational stems, and positive presuppositions) and inquiry categories (importance, under what conditions, source, data, beliefs, values). Example: "I'm curious about that assumption. Whose is it? Help me to understand more—what are some reasons that you value it highly?"
- Individuals inquire about posted assumptions in Round-Robin fashion

TIME:	GROUP SIZE:	MATERIALS:
15–25 minutes	Rearrange into groups of 4-6	Sentence strips large enough for one sentence that other group members can easily read

WHAT: **Working Agreements**

WHY: Creating and maintaining working agreements—what some groups refer to as "norms"—offer groups agreed upon behaviors to lubricate group work. When the group becomes the keeper of the agreements, most problems disappear.

HOW: Sample working agreements may include some of the following:

- Demonstrate Mutual Respect. Respect people and ideas. Respecting others does not equate to agreeing with them.
- Employ Skillful Listening. Seek first to understand, then to be understood.
- Develop Sufficient Consensus. Work to understand all views, distinguish between dialogue and discussion, give each person an equal voice, and reach 80% agreement of those present to constitute consensus.

When working agreements are well established, the group understands that once set, these agreements are not negotiable and the facilitator and group members will seek every opportunity to ensure compliance while working to shift more responsibility to the group.

Tip: Connect the agenda (see, Chapter 2) to working agreements. Ask, "Given our agenda, to which working agreements might we pay special attention"?

TIME:	GROUP SIZE:	MATERIALS:
8–10 minutes	Any	Chart paper

WHAT: **Polarity Mapping**

WHY: Makes tensions visible, honors all voices, and results in decisions that maintain the best possible outcomes of each potential solution while minimizing the negative effects of each. As a result, persons with different view points understand one another. The resolution is the best fit for the conflicting offers and generates a resolution most likely to reach a desired goal and utilize the strengths of each position.

HOW: Draw a four-quadrant box (see below) on chart paper, and do the following:

- Identify an ongoing chronic issue.
- Identify a key polarity. Some examples are work and home; individual and team; stability and change; independence and interdependence.
- Agree on value-neutral names for each of the poles.

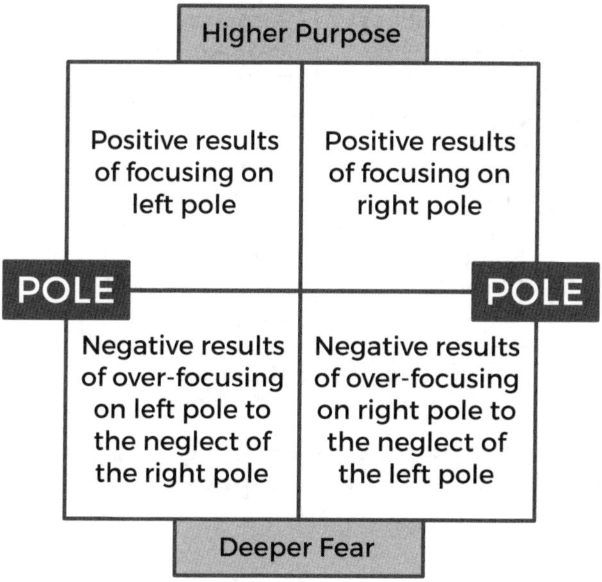

- Write the pole names on the map.
- Brainstorm content for each quadrant.
- Agree on a name for the higher purpose and deeper fear. Naming purpose and fear integrates oppositional views and provides a reason to manage the tension between the two views.
- Facilitate a conversation so members can view and explore the dilemma as a whole and with various perspectives. Empathetically paraphrase what participants say, so all know that they are being understood.
- Develop strategies for realizing the upsides of both poles while avoiding the downside of each pole.

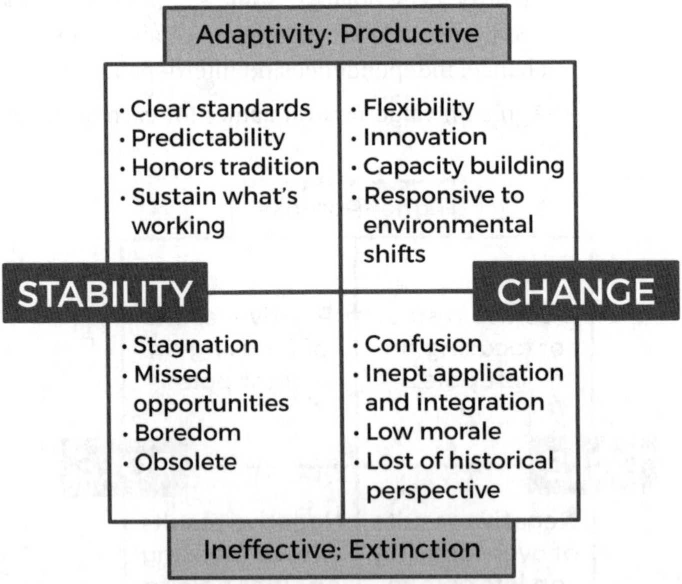

TIME:	GROUP SIZE:	MATERIALS:
40 minutes	6-12	Chart paper with Polarity Map

Reflecting

1. As you reflect upon your personal history with dealing with conflict, what are you becoming more aware of about what drives your reactions and methods?
2. To be curious rather than furious—which is part of the mindset to not let a conflict go to waste—can be demonstrated in your use of paraphrasing and then saying "Say more about that." When you self-assess your conflict capabilities, what is the next step for your own development?
3. What is the existing state and desired state of the group's conflict IQ? What resources will be beneficial? (See Desired State Map in Tools for Facilitators on page 86.)

Try This

1. Demonstrate conflict aikido with a co-learner: Place your palms against your partner's palms and apply light pressure. Have your partner role-play yelling at you while you push back against their palms and yell back. Stop, take a breath. Set an intention to seek understanding first, then reconnect palm to palm. As your partner again role-plays an angry outburst, listen carefully and paraphrase, being careful to add no pressure to your palms. As your partner continues, keep paraphrasing, while offering no physical resistance with your palms, gently backing up if necessary.
2. Debrief the experience: What did you notice, both externally and internally? What about your partner? What lessons might this activity have for your conflict IQ?
3. Identify a personal polarity and create a polarity map. Reflect: What insights am I gaining? How might I use this with a group?

Looking Back/Looking Ahead

> Do others see as I do? The pieces were there and yet they seemed to fall together differently. Slowly, it became clear that by allowing oneself the space of being able to see differently, that which was fixed, unchanging and given began to crumble and new patterns emerged. There was a new reality...
> —Leonard J. Duhl, *The Holographic Paradigm*

Conflict naturally occurs among humans and everywhere else. It can serve to reveal existing problems that seen anew can provide opportunities. Conflict among humans is characterized by differing approaches to resolving conflict, many learned as children observing parents and others. Paramount to progress in conflict resolution is unified approaches so only one template or process is used at a time. Language is a significant factor in disagreements. Strategically used, it represents intentions to understand and conveys respect for others, along with their opinions and positions. Consensus is an action, not an event and gaining sufficient consensus—about 80% agreement for many groups—launches periods of application in which consensus is demonstrated by collective behaviors in a group. Conflicts about ideas, as long as discussions don't turn personal, are a characteristic of strong teams.

Addenda

ADDENDUM A
Virtual Presence: Generalizations
by Kendall Zoller Ph.D.

Succeeding and thriving in a virtual environment is not as simple as simply transferring what you do face-to-face. When shifting to a virtual environment, you need to use your skills in new ways.

The following generalizations are presented for those of you who will use a virtual presence with your colleagues and students. The statements are brief and the intentions are two-fold:

1. Have you think about using your skills in new ways virtually, and
2. Increase your awareness of virtual platforms.

Virtual generalizations:

1. **The camera is the person.** When we want to make eye contact with participants, we have to look at our camera. Just like actors in a movie or TV show, when they look at the camera they are connecting to you. To replicate that connection in virtual meetings and sessions, look at the camera.
2. **Pausing can look like a frozen screen.** Ensure the audience knows you are pausing and not frozen by a poor connection. This can be done in many ways, including:
   a. announcing you are pausing;
   b. when pausing, moving slightly and continuously.

3. **Be seen as if you are in person.** Many of us know how we look on camera is not how we look live. To increase congruence, place your camera at eye level or slightly above. This mimics how people see you in real life.

4. **Animate your presence.** When virtual, animate more. Move towards and away from the camera. Smile larger, laugh louder. A monotone voice can be numbing when emanating from a computer screen. Mix it up.

5. **Camera perspective flattens depth perception, so adjust your gestures.** To make it look more congruent, place your gestures closer to your face when online. Practice and watch yourself to see what gestures you like best. Then use those when online.

6. **Moving in the viewing box is not moving in the room.** We move in face-to-face meetings, and we should move when online. Watch yourself as you move from side-to-side as well as from front to back. We can use our movements to shift content, ask questions, and create a location to signal time for thinking.

7. **Virtual visibility is transient.** When you show an agenda in an online presentation, once you move past the slide, the information may be lost. To keep information in the virtual room, show the information every time you reference it. When face-to-face, place your agenda on chart paper.

8. **Silence is uncomfortable virtually.** When virtual, a 1 or 2 second silence can seem eternal and awkward. To avoid uncomfortable silence, call on people first then say you are going to pause to give the speaker time to organize thoughts. When people know what is coming, they tend to be less uncomfortable.

9. **Stand to breathe.** Many of you stand when leading a meeting or professional development session. Consider doing it when online, too. By standing you will breathe better and give yourself more oxygen and energy.

10. **Slow down.** When we're virtual, we know not everyone has high-speed connections. To avoid any jerkiness, move your gestures more slowly and speak with greater enunciation than you do in real life

ADDENDUM B
Giving Clear Directions Is Not as Simple as It Looks
by Robert Garmston and Carolyn McKanders

We've trained hundreds of bright, competent people to make presentations on a range of topics and discovered that giving directions is more complex than we first thought. Here are some things we've learned by whispering in the ear of a novice just before they gave a direction and from interviewing them and experts in the field about their thought processes.

Our first realization is that there are four domains for direction giving. First is the simple form that is used repeatedly with minor variations. "Turn to your neighbor and name the key points for you on this topic." This pattern can be memorized after a few uses. Next is what a presenter says when introducing directions from a prepared PowerPoint slide. Third is giving multistep directions without a chart or power point. Fourth, and the most complex, is working from scratch, designing directions for an activity when none exists.

Some aspects are common in the delivery of each of the types.

Getting Attention

Both Grinder (1993) and Zoller (2010) strongly advocate that attention should always be the first order of business. To gain the group's attention, the leader combines these features as follows:

- Stand upright with your head and body still using a calm and centered posture. Align your feet under your shoulders. Grinder and Zoller call this a credible stance.
- Use a frozen gesture—which universally communicates "be silent—more is coming". This might be a finger in the air, a palm directed at yourself or some other natural gesture congruent with the verbal message.
- Use a credible voice and a brief phrase such as "Please look this direction" to get attention. This voice form is one in which the tonal pattern is flat and tends to curl down at the end of the sentence. This pattern is universally perceived as, "This is important information, please attend to it."

- Remain still, freezing your posture, holding your position until almost all members are silent and focused.
- When the group is attentive and still, break eye contact, breathe and step into another space. Use a credible voice to give the appropriate direction.

Using a Prepared Slide

Give an oral overview before showing slides with several steps so people know where you are going. Most often, directions are digested best when one line of the slide is revealed at a time, giving the presenter time to elaborate. Occasionally the first item will call for members to locate materials or arrange for a new partner. When this is the case, have members execute the first direction before showing the next steps. When the direction is something like *find a new partner,* include a simple initial task to minimize waiting or wasted time. For example: *Find a new partner and introduce yourself.* The last step in direction-giving should be a check for understanding. "What questions might you have about how to do this well?" is well phrased. "Do you have any questions?" is not. Leave the directions slide on the screen while the group begins its work. Remove the slide when no longer needed for guidance.

Managing Multistep Directions

If there are subsets to directions, the facilitator should use a visual paragraph for maximum congruence. In this pattern the facilitator gives the first direction, pauses, breaks eye contact by dropping their head, moves to a new spot, looks up, and gives the next direction. This pattern can be used for up to four stages in direction giving. Imagine the following statements (with expanded information for each) delivered with the visual paragraph after each of the first three directions. Figure 1 shows what might be said while giving multistep directions in a meeting or a classroom.

Figure 1: Supporting Multistep Directions Visually

Directions in a Meeting	Directions in a Classroom
• First you will brainstorm. • Next you will clarify. • Third you will advocate. • And finally you will rank what is most important to you.	• Take out your social studies book. • Turn to page 67. • Scan the odd numbered questions. • Write your answers to these questions in complete sentences.

A middle-school teacher in Portland, Oregon, stresses the combination of verbal and written instructions. He writes, "The general pattern for me is to write the instructions out on the board, instead of prewriting. (The process feels more organic and incorporates wait time into the overall process.) I then read the written instructions aloud and ask for questions. Subsequent questions that deal with instructions that have already been given (the inevitable, 'What page?,' 'What are we supposed to write?,' 'What number are we doing?' litany) are dealt with nonverbally. I usually just point to the board, maybe holding up fingers to reference a step number. I find the second part is crucial to helping learners learn to be good instruction followers, giving them the opportunity to practice 'guided self-reliance' if there is such a phrase" (Ferguson 2013).

We were surprised to learn that the thinking processes that support direction-giving are incredibly complex. At the simplest level, they include guidelines such as using declarative statements and a minimum number of words. Another level regards a direction-giving map we learned when interviewing Bruce Wellman, a noted professional developer who seems to effortlessly give profoundly direct and effective directions.

> This is described in Garmston and Zimmerman (2014) as follows:
>
> When introducing processes in which the group is to engage, the facilitator employs the what-why-how pattern. While each is important for the group to do its best work, the **why**—the rationale for the process is most important. When members understand the reasons for a process—how it will serve them—potential resistance is reduced and participation is more purposeful.

What –"The next step is to brainstorm."

Why – "As you know, the purpose of brainstorming is to get as many ideas on the table as possible. Questions or comments derail the process leading to a more limited and less useful list."

How – "I will record the ideas on this chart paper. When you raise your hand I will give you a number to place you in a queue so you know you will have a turn and not worry about being able to add your idea. If you have a question or comment, hang onto it. We will come back to it at the next step."

The fourth type of direction-giving, which is the most difficult, regards composing directions where none exist.

A Model for Designing Directions from Scratch

Some readers might like to think about how they would go about composing directions to participants to *explain their reasoning about the importance of consulting and coaching in supporting new teachers.* When you think about how you do this, you probably notice that you've gone allocentric—attempting to hear the instructions as your participants might hear them. Let's assume that the group is familiar with definitions related to the example above as Wikipedia offers them.

Consultation: to assist an individual or group of individuals to clarify and address immediate concerns by following a systematic problem-solving process.

Coaching: to enhance a person's competencies in a specific skill area by providing a process of observation, reflection, and action.

What we noticed when we examined our thinking was that we had to also define *reasoning.* If we wanted participants to dialogue, engage, and learn from one another, we might use the word *explore* in the directions. *Pairs: Explore the benefits of consulting and coaching for new teachers.* We might wonder what difference the word "for" or "to" new teachers might make. If, on the other hand, we desired a conversation that activated prior knowledge with greater specificity, we might develop a scaffold that begins with what we meant by *reasoning.* Such a scaffold might involve rewording the directions to *compare and contrast* the importance of consulting and coaching.

Pairs:

1. Compare and contrast the benefits of consulting and coaching for new teachers.
2. List the benefits of consulting.
3. List the benefits of coaching.
4. List the limitations of each.
5. Compare and contrast your findings.
6. Given the above, summarize your thinking about the relative importance of each.

Now with this first draft, we would seek to reduce the number of words while maintaining clarity.

Pairs: Compare and contrast consulting and coaching benefits for new teachers:

1. Make two lists. Record the benefits of each.
2. Record the limitations of each.
3. Identify what is same and different.
4. Write a statement concise enough to fit on a sticky note summarizing your conclusions.

The Potentially Pernicious Pronoun

What separates a good presenter or facilitator from an expert, is the use of pronouns. For some, it is difficult to replace the habit of saying, "I want you to look this direction," with phrases like "Please turn and look this way for next steps." The difference? In the first the leader is asking members to respond out of relationship serving the presenter—appropriate in the lexicon for a primary teacher, but not a person working with adults. Since we presume that an overarching goal of professional development is fostering a sense of equality in a training or meeting room, and supporting norms of autonomy, self-directedness and self-monitoring, we advise careful scripting of pronouns in giving directions.

Who you as facilitator are in relationship to the group should inform your use of pronouns. If you are a member of a group who has stepped up to facilitate the work may well be "ours." If you are external to the group, referring to the work as "ours" may carry inferences that interfere with the clarity of the group's work and its development. Compare these two statements: "Here is what I want you to do next." or "Listen carefully as I describe this process." Again, the former tends to infantilize the group, while the latter acknowledges them as responsible adults. Begin a list of phrases you want to incorporate when you give directions. You can start with these: "Your next steps are," "This process has three phases," "Take a moment to complete your thoughts and prepare to share your ideas with the group."

The Final Step

Finally, attend to the presentation of the direction itself. We've learned to mentally rehearse just before we give a direction. Sometimes we have scripted what we will say. Other times we simply stand in the space in which we are about to speak and put the words in our head before we talk. If during the directions we notice we have slipped and used an unintended pronoun, we stop, correct ourselves, and tell the group why. This transparency is valued not only because it equalizes the relationship—we are all learners here—but also because it teaches leadership principles.

Conclusion

Giving clear directions is a fundamental task for teachers, presenters, meeting facilitators, and anyone who works with groups. Complexities still exist, even when working with predeveloped directions on PowerPoints. The leader must still get the group's attention and orient participants regarding the task ahead. What-why-how is a fundamental part of this. So much of this is contextual, so giving directions, even for the most experienced of us, will always be a challenge.

References and Resources

Abrams, J. (2009). *Having Hard Conversations.* Thousand Oaks, CA: Corwin Press.

Bateson, G. (2000). *Steps to an Ecology of Mind: Collected Essays in Anthropology, Psychiatry, Evolution, and Epistemology.* (Revised Edition). Chicago, IL: University of Chicago Press.

Berger, J. G. (2019). *Unlocking Leadership Mindtraps: How to Thrive in Complexity.* Stanford, CA: Stanford University Press.

Brown, B. (2018). *Dare to Lead: Brave Work. Tough Conversations. Whole Hearts.* NY: Random House.

Costa, A. & Garmston, R. (2016). *Cognitive Coaching: Developing Self-Directed Leaders and Learners.* (3rd ed). Lanham, MA: Rowman & Littlefield.

Crum, T. (1998). *The Magic of Conflict: Turning a Life of Work into a Work of Art.* NY: Simon and Schuster.

Crum, T. (2021). https://www.azquotes.com/author/77890-Thomas_Crum

Desmond-Harris, J. (Feb. 16, 2015). *What Exactly Is a Microaggression?* Vox Media. https://www.vox.com/2015/2/16/8031073/what-are-microaggressions

DiSalvo, D. (June 22, 2013). "The Brain Sees Even When You Don't." *Forbes.* https://www.forbes.com/sites/daviddisalvo/2013/06/22/your-brain-sees-even-when-you-dont/?sh=5e166f78116a

Donohoo, J. (2017). *Collective Efficacy: How Educators' Beliefs Impact Student Learning.* Thousand Oaks, CA: Corwin Press.

Duhigg, C. (Feb. 25, 2016). "What Google Learned from Its Quest to Build the Perfect Team." *The New York Times Magazine.*

Duhl, L. (1985). "Experiencing Holography." In Wilber, K. (Ed.), *The Holographic Paradigm and Other Paradoxes: Exploring the Leading Edge of Science.* Boulder, CO: New Science Library.

Dweck, C. (2016). "What Having a 'Growth Mindset' Actually Means." *Harvard Business Review.* Retrieved December 22, 2020. https://hbr.org/2016/01/what-having-a-growth-mindset-actually-means

Dweck, C. (2016). *Mindset: The New Psychology of Success.* NY: Ballantine Books.

Eden, D. (2018). "Charismatic Pygmalion: The Most Effective Leadership Combo." In Katz, I., Eilam-Shamir, G. R., Kark, & Berson, Y. (Eds.) *Leadership Now: Reflections on the Legacy of Boas Shamir (Monographs in leadership and management Book 9),* (pp. 109-123). Emerald Publishing Limited. https://doi.org/10.1108/S1479-357120180000009003

Edmondson, A. (2019). *The Fearless Organization: Creating Psychological Safety in the Workplace for Learning, Innovation, and Growth.* Hoboken, NJ: John Wiley & Sons, Inc.

Erickson, M. H. & Rossi, E. (Eds.). (1980). *Innovative Hypnotherapy: Collected Papers of Milton H. Erickson on Hypnosis.* NY: Irvington.

Ferguson, W. (2013). Written communication.

Flanagan, N. & Finger, J. (2005). *The Management Bible.* London: New Holland Pub Ltd.

Fredrickson, B. L. (2001). "The Role of Positive Emotions in Positive Psychology: The Broaden-and-Build Theory of Positive Emotions." *American Psychologist,* 56(3), 218–226. https://doi.org/10.1037/0003-066X.56.3.218

Fredrickson, B. L. (2009). *Positivity: Top-Notch Research Reveals the 3-to-1 Ratio That Will Change Your Life.* NY: Crown.

Fredrickson, B. L. (2013). "Updated Thinking on Positivity Ratios." *American Psychologist,* 68(9), 814–822. doi: 10.1037/a0033584

Garmston, R. (2018) *The Astonishing Power of Story Telling: Leading, Teaching, and Transforming in a New Way.* Thousand Oaks, CA: Corwin

Garmston, R. & Zimmerman, D. (2013). *Lemons to Lemonade: Resolving Problems in Meetings, Workshops, and PLCs.* Thousand Oaks, CA: Corwin Press.

Garmston, R. J. & Wellman, B. M. (2016). *The Adaptive School: A Sourcebook for Developing Collaborative Groups.* (3rd ed.). Lanham, Maryland: Rowman & Littlefield.

Goddard, R. D., Hoy, W. K. & Hoy, A. W. (April 1, 2004). "Collective Efficacy Beliefs: Theoretical Developments, Empirical Evidence, and Future Directions." *Educational Researcher,* 33(3), 3–13. https://doi.org/10.3102/0013189X033003003

Gottman, J., et al. (2002). *The Mathematics of Marriage: Dynamic Nonlinear Models.* MA: MIT.

Grant, A. (2021). *Think Again: The Power of Knowing What You Don't Know.* NY: Viking.

Grinder, M. (1993). *ENVoY: Your Personal Guide to Classroom Success.* Battle Ground WA: Michael Grinder & Associates.

Grinder, M. (2008). *The Science of Nonverbal Communication* (1st Edition). Battleground, WA: Michael Grinder and Associates.

Hammond, Z. L. (2015). *Culturally Responsive Teaching and The Brain.* Thousand Oaks, CA: Corwin.

Hanifan, O. (2020). *The 7 Key Traits of an Excellent Facilitator.* Mentimeter.com. https://www.mentimeter.com/blog/great-leadership/the-7-key-traits-of-an-excellent-facilitator

Howard, T., et al. (2019). *All Students Must Thrive: Transforming Schools to Combat Toxic Stressors and Cultivate Critical Wellness.* Rexford, NY: International Center for Leadership in Education.

Johnson, B. (2020). *And: Making a Difference by Leveraging Polarity, Paradox or Dilemma (Volume One: Foundations).* Amherst, MA: HRD Press.

Keltner, D. (Oct. 2016). "Don't Let Power Corrupt You." *Harvard Business Review.*

Khanna, D. (Sept. 24, 2019). "So, What Are You? Dealing with Microaggressions at Work." *The Seattle Times.*

Kwong, E. (Host). (July 15, 2020). "Understanding Unconscious Bias" Short Wave. *NPR.* https://www.npr.org/2020/07/14/891140598/understanding-unconscious-bias

Leonard, G. (1968). *Education and Ecstasy.* New York: Delacorte Press.

Lindsay, D. B., Martinez, R. S. & Lindsay, R. B. (2007). *Culturally Proficient Coaching: Supporting Educators to Create Equitable Schools.* Thousand Oaks, CA: Corwin.

Losada, M. & Heaphy, E. (2004). "The Role of Positivity and Connectivity in the Performance of Business Teams: A Nonlinear Dynamics Model." *American Behavioral Scientist,* 47(6), 740–765.

Miravia.com. (2002, 2008). "ChartArt." https://www.miravia.com/products/chartart-combo-2

Pinker, S. (Jan. 13, 2008). "The Moral Instinct." *The New York Times Magazine.*

Rock, D. (2009). *Your Brain at Work: Strategies for Overcoming Distraction, Regaining Focus, and Working Smarter All Day Long.* NY: HarperCollins Publishers.

Rosenthal, R. & Jacobson, L. (1968). *Pygmalion in the Classroom: Teacher Expectation and Pupils' Intellectual Development.* NY: Holt, Rinehart & Winston.

Rudd, T. (Feb. 5, 2014). "Racial Disproportionality in School Discipline: Implicit Bias Is Heavily Implicated" (Kirwan Institute Issue Brief), 1-8. http://kirwaninstitute.osu.edu/wp-content/uploads/2014/02/racial-disproportionality-schools-02.pdf

Seehausen, M., Kazzer, P., Bajbouj, M. & Prehn, K. (2012). "Effects of Empathic Paraphrasing—Extrinsic Emotion Regulation in Social Conflict." *Frontiers in Psychology,* 3(482). https://doi.org/10.3389/fpsyg.2012.00482

Seib, G. F. (Nov. 21, 2008). "In Crisis, Opportunity for Obama." *The Wall Street Journal.*

Wellman, B. & Lipton, L. (2017). *Data-Driven Dialogue: A Facilitator's Guide to Collaborative Inquiry,* Burlington, VT: Miravia LLC.

Wing Sue, D. (Posted November 17, 2010). "Micro aggressions: More Than Just Race," *Psychology Today.*

Woolley, A., Chabris, C., Pentland, A., Hashmi, and Malone, T. (2010). "Evidence for a Collective Intelligence Factor in the Performance of Human Groups." *Science,* 330(6004): 686-688.

Workable.com. (2021). "What Are the Types of Diversity?" https://resources.workable.com/hr-terms/the-types-of-diversity

Zimmerman, D., Roussin, J., & Garmston, R. (2020). *Transforming Teamwork: Cultivating Collaborative Cultures.* Thousand Oaks, CA: Corwin Press.

Zoller, K. (2007). *Nonverbal Patterns of Teachers from Five Countries: Results from the TIMSS-R Video Study.* (Publication No. 3283067). Doctoral Dissertation, California State University Fresno and University of California Davis. ProQuest Dissertations Publishing.

Zoller, K. & Landry, C. (2010). *The Choreography of Presenting.* Thousand Oaks, CA: Corwin Press.

Index